TO BE CONTINUED?

TO BE CONTINUED?

Are the Miraculous Gifts
for Today?

Samuel E. Waldron

Calvary Press Publishing · Merrick, New York
www.calvarypress.com

Calvary Press Publishing
2005 Merrick Road, #341
Merrick, New York 11566

ISBN 1-879737-58-2

1. Christian Life 2. Charismatic Movement 3. Miracles
4. Contemporary Issues 5. Applied Theology

Graphic Design Services: AnthonyRotolo.com

Manufactured in the USA
1 2 3 4 5 6 7 8 9 10 04 05 06 07 08

Praise for *To Be Continued?*

"Cessationism (the view that miraculous spiritual gifts pertained only to the apostolic era) has fallen out of favor in recent years. That's an especially untimely development in an era when so many churches have been disrupted by charismatic confusion—while false miracles and questionable spiritual gifts abound. The primary argument against cessationism seems to be that if there's no decisive proof-text stating that the miraculous gifts have ceased, and no single passage from which a cessationist theology can be exegetically established, then cessationism must be summarily rejected. But the cessation of the miraculous gifts, the passing of the apostolic era, and the closing of the biblical canon are all interrelated truths, dealing with the very same theological issues. To claim that the spiritual gifts are still operative is as spiritually dangerous as believing that the canon of Scripture is still open. The history of the modern charismatic movement furnishes ample proof that this is true. Pastor Waldron does an excellent job of establishing the biblical and theological basis for historic cessationism, bringing clarity and sanity to an issue that has too long been dominated by emotion and muddled thinking."
PHIL JOHNSON , DIRECTOR OF GRACE TO YOU

"*First*, this book is readable, well organized, and concise. No one should put it down because they have found it too opaque. *Second*, the doctrinal pertinence of it does not depend on any of the immediately relevant issues, such as Pentecostalism, charismatic presence, or third wave. It gives quite striking discussions of issues relative to those movements, but it stands as an important piece of theological reasoning in itself. A clear and biblically fulsome development of the purpose, location, and rationale of divine revelation must help every believer in his love for Scripture as well as expand his confidence in the evidence provided within the Bible itself for its defensibility as a word from God. *Third*, you have given your reasoning in the context of careful biblical exegesis in a redemptive-historical context. *Fourth*, the book's fragrance is one of kindness as well as firmness toward brothers that you recognize as equally fervent in their desire to live according to biblical truth. Sam Waldron treats eveyone with respect and grants them a serious hearing. I look forward to the book's appearance and will recommend it widely, particularly to my friends in the 'third wave.'"
TOM J. NETTLES, PROFESSOR, SOUTHERN THEOLOGICAL SEMINARY

"The argument of Sam Waldron's book is simple and straightforward, yet with far-reaching implications. In essence, he argues (and I think quite persuasively) from the absence of Apostles to the absence of all miraculous gifts. He does this by displaying the connection between Apostles, prophets, tongues-speakers, miracle-workers, and infallible, special revelation. His tone is irenic and respectful of those he differs with, and thus exemplary. In a day when Continuationism is gaining approval in high-profile places, it is my hope that the Lord will use this book to fortify some and challenge others to base all doctrine and practice on sound exegesis and clear theological implication."
RICHARD C. BARCELLOS , PASTOR, AUTHOR OF *IN DEFENSE OF THE DECALOGUE*

"The issue of miraculous gifts represents one of the continuing controversies in modern evangelicalism. Writing as a dedicated Cessationist, Sam Waldron offers a generous but clear argument against those who argue for the continuation of these gifts in the church today. Sam Waldron is a careful scholar and a caring pastor, and his argument reflects both of these qualities. Even those who disagree with his analysis will be stretched and informed by Waldron's careful study."
R. ALBERT MOHLER, JR., PRESIDENT, SOUTHERN BAPTIST THEOLOGICAL SEMINARY

INTRODUCTION

CHAPTER 1

THE QUESTION, THE READERS, THE ARGUMENT

OF THE QUESTION

This little book does not pretend to be a comprehensive discussion of Pentecostalism, the Charismatic Movement, or the Third Wave. Many such discussions, both pro and con, both good and bad, already exist. It addresses only one of the teachings normally associated with these increasingly popular and important movements in Christianity and in the world: the teaching that may be succinctly described as Continuationism.[1]

Continuationism is the teaching that (at least some of) the miraculous gifts assumed and described in the Bible ought to continue in the church and, in fact, do continue to be given to the church. The words in parentheses above must be carefully noted. At times—and in some of its popular forms—Continuationism and Continuationists teach that there are no Apostles of Christ today.[2] They do, however, usually believe that prophets, tongues-speakers, and miracle-workers continue to be given by Christ to His church.

If it seems inconsistent to admit that certain miraculous gifts (Apostles of Christ) have ceased, while maintaining that others continue, this is because it is! Here I must admit that I am a Cessationist and will be defending in the following pages a form of Cessationism. Cessationism is the opposite of Continuationism. It teaches that all the miraculous gifts have ceased to be given to the church today. When I say I will be defending a form of Cessationism, I mean I will argue that, though the miraculous gifts have ceased to be given, this does not mean that God never performs miracles or supernatural works in the world today. My form of Cessationism argues that miraculous gifts, on the one hand, and miracles, on the other hand, are distinct and that the Bible teaches the cessation of the miraculous gifts, but not all miracles. God did not lock Himself out of the world when the last Apostle of Christ died or when the last book of the canon of Scripture was written. He is still perfectly able to do miracles in the world. I believe He occasionally does so. This, however, is a different thing than saying He still gives miraculous gifts—miraculously gifted people—to the church.

This distinction between miraculously gifted people and miracles is somewhat controversial. A Continuationist may reply to this distinction, that "strictly speaking to be an Apostle is an office, not a gift."[3] Such a Continuationist might say that in the New Testament a clear distinction is made between the gift and the person who has the gift.[4] Thus, such a Continuationist may find the argument of this book unconvincing on the grounds that I confuse person or office and gift. Yet in the key passages on this subject, Paul does not maintain the distinction upon which such a Continuationist insists. Ephesians 4:11, for instance, identifies the gifts Christ gives (mentioned in Ephesians 4:8) as apostles, prophets, evangelists, and pastor-teachers. Similarly in 1 Corinthians 12:28-29 apostles, prophets, and teachers occur in lists of what are evidently gifts.[5]

It is interesting that the very proponent of Continuationism whom I just cited, admits in another place that "the New Testament pictures a permanent possession of spiritual gifts." He goes on to say: "Paul says that some people have titles that describe a continuing function."[6] What this Continuationist seems to miss, however, is that it is just for these reasons that those given the gifts necessary to being an apostle or a prophet may themselves be called miraculous gifts.

Paul's example and Grudem's admission justify my speaking in this book of the gifts of apostles, prophets, tongues-speakers, and miracle-workers. They also justify the distinction between miracle-workers and miracles assumed in the following pages. A miracle-worker is a person permanently gifted to do miracles.[7] God may do miracles without doing them through miracle-workers. Hence, there may be miracles in the world today without there being miracle-workers. For instance, the church may gather to pray for a brother with a terminal cancer. The elders of the church may gather to his sickbed to pray for him. At his next medical examination this brother may be found to be free of cancer. This healing may properly be called supernatural and even miraculous, yet neither the church, nor the elders claim the gift of healing. No one among them claims to be a faith-healer. No one in this church or its eldership ever again has a similar involvement in, or experience of, miraculous healing. In such a situation, there is a miracle, but no miracle-worker.

Why have I chosen to address only the issue of Continuationism in this book? It seems to me the discussions related to Pentecostalism and the Charismatic movement have entered a new stage. Earlier important discussions of these movements have focused on their claims with regard to the baptism of the Spirit and the so-called doctrine of subsequence: the teaching that subsequent to conversion, and by fulfilling certain further conditions, a Christian must be baptized by the Spirit. This subsequent baptism of the Spirit was variously thought to provide the Christian with greater holiness, power, or assurance. This turning point was usually thought to be marked by the experience of speaking in tongues.[8] With the arrival of the so-called Third Wave (the first two having been Pentecostalism and the Charismatic movement), the focus of doctrinal attention has altered. While Pentecostalism and the Charismatic movement continue to teach their distinctive views of the baptism of the Spirit, the Third Wave has largely given up the idea that the baptism of the Spirit occurs subsequent to conversion. It continues, however, to teach that preaching of the gospel should be accompanied by the exercise of miraculous gifts.[9]

It is important to notice that it is in the form of the Third Wave that the movements associated with the continuation of the miraculous gifts have penetrated most deeply into the evangelicalism.[10] Other events at the same time also served to raise the influence of these movements in evangelical circles. Most important of these may have been D. Martyn Lloyd-Jones' embrace of a form of the doctrine of subsequence. Intentionally or not, this implied support for some form of Continuationism.[11]

For these reasons, while issues related to the baptism of the Spirit have receded into the background, Continuationism has begun to exercise a surprising influence on evangelicals.[12] Not only have many embraced Continuationism, but also a significant number have decided to take an open, but cautious approach to the issue. It seems to me, therefore, that the argument developed here against Continuationism is very timely. It is not original to me, but I do hope the reader will judge its cogency and power to be displayed in a fresh way.

TO THE READERS
Speaking of those I hope will read this book, let me address a word to three distinct groups of readers.

To my Continuationist friends who read this book, let me admit that I fear you have already defeated us Cessationists in the propaganda battle. Continuationism sounds so much more bright and hopeful than the dour and sour sound of Cessationism. In a day where it is so important to be positive (Insert here a smiley-face!) and so bad to be negative (as in "Don't be so negative!"), Continuationism sounds more positive than Cessationism. All I plead here is that you not think that because you may have won the propaganda battle (by being pro-miraculous gifts, while others are anti-miraculous gifts) that you have won the biblical battle. Sounds—as well as looks—may be deceiving. The negative warnings and commands of the Bible (Take care lest...! Thou shalt not...!) offer much more hope and a much brighter future than the very positive false prophets who say, "Peace, peace, where there is no peace." Even so, Cessationism offers a perspective that calls the church to take its stand, not on the sandy foundation of continuing miraculous gifts, but on the mighty and majestic written Word of God.

Let me also say something on this issue to my friends who are open, but cautious on this issue.[13] In this phraseology the tide runs against Cessationism even more strongly than in the contrast with Continuationism. You are open, but cautious. The conclusion must be, then, that I am closed and reckless? To be open and cautious is to be tolerant, but judicious. Those who hold Cessationism must, therefore, be intolerant and imprudent. I must admit that for my side this common terminology seems to be a lost cause.

I am, of course, only half-serious, but I am trying to make an important point. There is certainly no desire to impugn the integrity of your opinions on this issue. I do urge you, however, to make very sure that you do not come to superficial conclusions on this important issue merely because the artfully-coined phrase, open but cautious, makes other positions seem injudicious. Consider carefully the argument in the pages that follow. See if the toleration of Continuationism by the open, but cautious position does not allow dangerous principles to run rampant in evangelical circles.

Finally, let me address a word or two to my Cessationist allies and readers. I have tread my own path at several points in the argument that follows, occasionally diverging from standard or at least common positions of other defenders of Cessationism.[14] I have not done this to be novel. Indeed, I am not aware that any of my positions are novel. These positions have been taken because I believe our stance is so crucial that it deserves the most honest and careful exegetical support I can give it. Let me also say that I believe the way in which I have developed the argument for Cessationism has much to commend it. I think the bastion and beginning, the clearest evidence and starting-point, of our position is the cessation of the gift of Apostles of Christ. Conversely, the fatal flaw and unraveling point of the Continuationist position is its insensitivity to and neglect of the implications of an historically limited apostolate. I hope my emphasis on this point will help you in the defense and propagation of truth.

ABOUT THE ARGUMENT

It will assist the clarity of the following argument for the reader if I preview it here. While I hope the following pages will not be dense, the argument is, I think, tightly reasoned. To fully appreciate it, the line of thought must be clear to the reader.

My argument is as follows:

The New Testament makes clear that Apostles of Christ are not given to the church today; they lived only in the first century. We know for sure, therefore, that one gift, and that the greatest gift, has ceased to be given. This clear New Testament teaching provides a vital premise for the argument against Continuationism. Unless it wishes to contradict the plainest evidence, Continuationism cannot claim that there is no difference in the gifts given to the church today and the gifts given to the church in the first century.

Prophets in the Old Testament were a clearly identified and regulated institution that contributed prominently to the formation of the Old Testament canon. There is no reason to think New Testament prophecy is fundamentally different than Old Testament prophecy. There is, in fact, every reason to think it is fundamentally the same. Since biblical prophets were foundational (Eph. 2:20), infallible, and canonical, then prophecy has ceased.

Tongues-speaking is substantially equivalent to prophecy according to the New Testament. According to 1 Corinthians 14:5 tongues plus interpretation equals prophecy. As such, tongues-speaking—like prophecy—has ceased.

Miracle-workers performed miraculous signs intended to vindicate the divine authority of the messages with which they were entrusted. It is impossible, therefore, to suppose there could be miracle-workers today without supposing they were either apostles or prophets bringing inspired messages from God. Since we have already concluded that the miraculous gifts of apostles and prophets have ceased, we must also conclude that Christ no longer gives miracle-workers to the church. This assertion, however, does not require the conclusion that God Himself does no miracles today.

A picture—in this case a diagram—is worth a thousand words. The following diagram illustrates the Cascade Argument against Continuationism.

THE CASCADE ARGUMENT

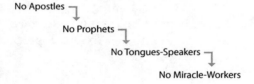

The chapters of this book outline the development of The Cascade Argument. I hope this outline strikes you as straightforward. It is my hope that you will not only be able to follow the argument, but that you will be convinced by it.

1   I have been cautioned by a good and learned friend that the term Continuationism may be a somewhat novel and even offensive way of describing the
position that I am criticizing. Since I was intending to be neither novel nor
offensive, I was surprised by these comments. Through a search of the internet,
I determined that a few others before me have described the position I am addressing as Continuationism. I certainly do not intend this descriptive word to
be in any way offensive. If I am willing to be described as a Cessationist, it does
not seem unkind to me to describe my "loyal opposition" as Continuationists.

2   Wayne Grudem, *Systematic Theology: An Introduction to Biblical Doctrine*
(Grand Rapids: Zondervan, 1994), p. 911.

3   Grudem, *Systematic Theology*, p.1020. Grudem's Systematic Theology seems
to be having a broad (and deserved) usefulness in evangelical circles. In this
work, however, he defends Continuationism. For these reasons I will interact
with him frequently in the following pages.

4   Ibid.

5   In fact, in 1 Corinthians 12:29 the word miracles actually comes to mean miracle-workers and is so translated by the KJV, NKJV, ASV, and NASB. The NIV,
RSV, and NRSV give the translation, "Do all work miracles?"

6   Grudem, *Systematic Theology*, p.1025. Cf. the rest of his excellent discussion
of this matter.

7   I am not implying that a miracle-worker can do miracles any time he or she
wishes, any more than a prophet might prophesy any time he wishes. A prophet is one attested as someone through whom God gives prophecy. A miracle-
worker is a person known as one through whom God does miracles.

8   Frederick Dale Bruner, *A Theology of the Holy Spirit* (Grand Rapids: Eerdmans,
1970) is perhaps the most important critical study of Pentecostalism and the
Charismatic movement. He focuses his massive study almost exclusively on
the baptism of the Spirit and the doctrine of subsequence. Comparatively little
is said about the continuation of the miraculous gifts.

9   Grudem, *Systematic Theology*, p.763, has an excellent discussion and explanation of the change in doctrinal focus that accompanied the rise of the Third
Wave.

10   C. Peter Wagner (deeply associated with the Third Wave) taught at that quint-
essential evangelical institution, Fuller Seminary.

11   The disturbances caused in British Evangelicalism by D. Martyn Lloyd-Jones'
embracing a form of the doctrine of subsequence and the seeming approval
it gave to the other distinctive features of the Charismatic movement is tell-
ingly reflected in Donald Macleod's *The Spirit of Promise* (Ross-shire, Scotland:

Christian Focus Publications, 1986). Lloyd-Jones related this subsequent experience to assurance of salvation and power in preaching.

12   *Are Miraculous Gifts for Today? Four Views*, ed. Wayne A. Grudem (Grand Rapids: Zondervan, 1996) illustrates this influence. The Cessationist view (defended by Richard B. Gaffin Jr.) finds itself surrounded by the Open But Cautious view (defended by Robert L. Saucy), The Third Wave view (defended by C. Samuel Storms), and The Pentecostal/Charismatic view (defended by Douglas A. Oss). Saucy and Storms are well-known evangelicals.

13   In *Are Miraculous Gifts for Today? Four Views*, ed. Wayne A. Grudem, the Open But Cautious view is one of the four views and is defended by Robert L. Saucy. Grudem, *Systematic Theology*, remarks: "We should also realize that there is a large 'middle' group with respect to this question, a group of 'mainstream evangelicals' who are neither charismatics or Pentecostals on the one hand, nor 'cessationists' on the other hand, but are simply undecided, and unsure if the question can be decided from Scripture."

14   Note, for instance, my treatment of the Continuationist argument from 1 Corinthians 13:9-10 in Chapter Four.

PART 1

APOSTLES

CHAPTER 2

THE APOSTLES: WHO WERE THEY?

INTRODUCTION

The Pentecostal, Charismatic, and Third Wave movements have been wildly successful and have literally changed the face of Christianity in the world.[1] Christians who are not Continuationists could probably provide many reasons unflattering to Continuationists as to why the Charismatic movement has been so popular. Here, however, I want to raise what may be a more difficult question for such Christians. Are there positive, or we might even say godly or good reasons, why the Charismatic movement appeals to genuine Christians?

I believe we who are not Continuationists should recognize at least two positive appeals of Continuationism. It takes the New Testament seriously, and it is unashamedly supernaturalist in its understanding of Christianity. Let me explain.

First, Continuationism takes the New Testament seriously. It sees miraculous gifts like prophets, tongues-speakers, and miracle-workers in the New Testament church and asks why the church today should not be just like the New Testament church. Certainly, no conservative Christian should fault Continuationists for wanting to take their Bibles seriously.

Second, this viewpoint is unashamedly supernaturalist. It sees in the Bible a God in heaven who is free to perform miracles, and it utterly refuses to feel any embarrassment about this miracle-working God. In our Post-Enlightenment age, both evangelical embarrassment over miracles and liberal rejection of miracles have been all too common.[2]

Now if we claim to take the New Testament as our authority, and if we claim to be unembarrassed supernaturalists, then Continuationism must be taken seriously. We must ask the question: How can we answer these positive appeals and arguments of Continuationism? Are we being inconsistent and failing to take our Bibles seriously when they speak of extraordinary gifts in the New Testament church? Or is there some sort of doctrinal line or scriptural filter that prevents the miraculous gifts from crossing into the church today? If so, what is its nature?

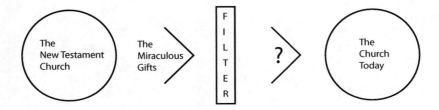

This series of questions brings us to the first miraculous gift or extraordinary office with which we must deal in these studies, the office or gift of apostles. Just as we call the office of pastor, the pastorate, and the office of deacon, the diaconate, so also the office of apostle is called the apostolate. The apostolate suggests a doctrinal line or scriptural filter that must be drawn between the church of the New Testament period and the church of all later periods. It is crucial for many reasons that this distinction be made between the church of the New Testament and the church of later periods. When this line is drawn, it will greatly assist us in seeing why we need not think that the miraculous or extraordinary gifts are for today. Unfortunately, the prominence and distinctiveness of the apostolate in the New Testament is not generally recognized. Many passages and promises addressed first or even exclusively to the Apostles of Christ are spiritualized or devotionalized and applied to all Christians.

Have you ever heard the statements in 1 John 1:1-3 spiritualized and applied to all Christians? Read carefully, however, they are literally true only of the Apostles of Christ and a few other early disciples who actually touched, handled, saw, and heard our Lord.

> What was from the beginning, what we have heard, what we have seen with our eyes, what we have looked at and touched

with our hands, concerning the Word of Life. And the life was manifested, and we have seen and testify and proclaim to you the eternal life, which was with the Father and was manifested to us. What we have seen and heard we proclaim to you also, so that you too may have fellowship with us; and indeed our fellowship is with the Father, and with His Son Jesus Christ.

How often have you heard the promises of the Spirit in John 14-16 (which are given first and in some ways exclusively to the Apostles of Christ) applied without qualification to all Christians? Yet many of these promises clearly have as their primary meaning something that can only be true of Apostles. Take, for instance, John 15:26-27: "When the Helper comes, whom I will send to you from the Father, *that is* the Spirit of truth who proceeds from the Father, He will testify about Me, and you *will* testify also, *because you have been with Me from the beginning.*" (Emphasis mine).[3] This tendency among evangelicals not to recognize the centrality and distinctiveness of the apostolate in the New Testament (and rather to universalize, spiritualize, and devotionalize language that refers specifically to apostles) has contributed significantly to the appeal of Charismatic and Continuationist arguments to evangelicals.

Before beginning let me make several things clear. First of all, I recognize, and Cessationists in general should understand, that many Charismatics and Continuationists agree that no living Apostles of Christ inhabit the world today. Though not a few Charismatic groups do claim living apostles, and against such the following argument is particularly relevant, yet many, and perhaps most, Charismatics or Continuationists do not make such claims. This does not mean, however, that the ensuing argument for the cessation of the apostolate is irrelevant for such Continuationists. On the contrary, I intend to show that the admission that the apostolate has ceased is a fatal crack in the foundation of Continuationism.

The Biblical definition of Apostles
Fundamental to everything else we will study about apostles is the meaning of the word. Most readers of this book will remember what the word apostle means. An apostle is a "sent one." Both in Hebrew and Greek the word for an apostle is derived from the verb that means "to send."

Among the Jews, however, the word, *sjaliach*, "sent one," had attained a very specific meaning. Ridderbos notes, "Recent research has shown that the formal structure of the apostolate is derived from the Jewish legal system in which a person may be given the legal power to represent another. The one who has such power of attorney is called a Sjaliach (apostle). The uniqueness of this relationship is pregnantly expressed by the notion that the Sjaliach (apostle) of a man, is as the man himself."[4]

In the New Testament, the Greek word *apostle*[5] also possesses a similar technical meaning. Jesus Christ was his Father's Apostle (Heb. 3:1-2). Thus what Jesus said, His Father said (John 14:6-10). In a similar way, the Twelve are His Apostles (John 20:21). To receive Christ's Apostle is to receive Him (Matt. 10:40; John 13:20). Therefore, an apostle was one's legal representative. He possessed—to use modern parlance—power of attorney for someone else.

The Necessary Distinction Regarding Apostles

If an apostle is one's legal representative, then everything about the nature and authority of the office depends on whose legal representative he is. The representative or apostle of the President of the United States would possess a great authority. My representative or apostle would possess very little. Both the President's representative and my representative would be apostles. Yet their apostolic authority or office would differ greatly because of whom they represent.

This thought enables us to clear up something that may be the source of much confusion among Charismatics and other Christians. People ask, "Are there apostles today?" The first response to that question must be, "Apostles of whom?"

Let me explain. We must make a distinction in the New Testament between those who were Apostles of Christ (big-A apostles) and those who were simply apostles of the churches (small-A apostles). Apostles of Christ are Christ's direct, legal representatives. Apostles of the churches are the churches' legal representatives and only indirectly, and in a lesser sense, the representatives of Christ. You can see apostles of the churches mentioned in Philippians 2:25 and 2 Corinthians 8:23. In the sense of apostles of churches, apostles do exist today. A missionary sent out by a local church would be an apostle of that church. A representative sent to a meeting of an association of churches is another example of an apostle of that church. Such persons are apostles of the church that sends them. They are not, however, official apostles in the sense of being an Apostle of Christ.

Think of it this way: You may know that the New Testament uses the word *elder* sometimes simply to refer to an older man, but other times to refer to an office in the church. Compare 1 Tim. 5:1 with 5:17. You may also know that the New Testament uses the word deacon sometimes simply to refer to a servant or minister, but other times to refer to an office in the church. Compare 1 Tim. 4:6 with 3:8. Even so, sometimes the New Testament uses the word apostle simply to refer to a legal representative in general and other times to refer to those who were officially the legal representatives of Christ.

Therefore, when we read about apostles in the New Testament, we must not willy-nilly assume that we are always reading about Apostles of Christ. We may be reading about small-A apostles. For instance, sometimes Romans 16:7 is used to multiply all sorts of little-known Apostles of Christ in the New Testament church: "Greet Andronicus and Junias, my kinsmen and my fellow prisoners, who are outstanding among the apostles, who also were in Christ before me." For Continuationists, Andronicus and Junias then become a kind of suggestive proof for Apostles of Christ today. Andronicus and Junias may, however, be small-A apostles, missionaries of some local church or something else. There is also a second problem with this use of Andronicus and Junias: they may not be apostles in any sense at all. The verse could be translated, "Salute Andronicus and Junia, my kinsmen, and my fellowprisoners, who are of note among the apostles, who also were in Christ before me."[6] In other words, the verse may simply mean that Andronicus and Junias were recognized and esteemed by the Apostles of Christ and not that they were actually among the number of the Apostles of Christ.[7]

Indispensable Characteristics Of Apostles

In the New Testament, there are at least three indispensable characteristics of an Apostle of Christ (the big-A apostle). These characteristics were unique and limited to only a few men. They are further proof of the distinction between big-A and small-A apostles.

An Eye-witness Of The Resurrected Christ

The first of these indispensable characteristics of an Apostle of Christ was that he had to be an eyewitness of the resurrected Christ (Acts 1:22; 10:39-41; 1 Cor. 9:1).

Acts 1:22—Beginning with the baptism of John until the day that He was taken up from us—one of these must become a witness with us of His resurrection.

Acts 10:39—We are witnesses of all the things He did both in the land of the Jews and in Jerusalem. They also put Him to death by hanging Him on a cross. 40 God raised Him up on the third day and granted that He become visible, 41 not to all the people, but to witnesses who were chosen beforehand by God, that is, to us who ate and drank with Him after He arose from the dead.

1 Corinthians 9:1—Am I not free? Am I not an apostle? Have I not seen Jesus our Lord? Are you not my work in the Lord?

It is important here to emphasize that the eyes in question were physical eyes. Even Paul—the untimely born Apostle of Christ (1 Cor. 15:8)—could claim to have seen the resurrected Christ with his physical eyes. According to Acts 9:1-8, Paul both heard a physical voice and saw a physical light—the glory of the resurrected Lord Jesus. The men with Paul heard the voice.[8] The light was so real that it was apparently responsible for blinding Paul—a physical effect. In 1 Corinthians 15:1-11 Paul makes very clear that he is claiming the same kind of appearance to himself that the original apostles received (1 Cor. 15:7-8).

Why do I emphasize that seeing the resurrected Christ with one's physical eyes is so indispensable? The Old Testament distinguished between Moses and the prophets in just this way. In Numbers 12:1-4, we are told that Miriam and Aaron spoke against Moses. God, in Numbers 12:5-8, emphasizes the dignity of Moses as compared to even prophets.

Numbers 12:5 Then the LORD came down in a pillar of cloud and stood at the doorway of the tent, and He called Aaron and Miriam. When they had both come forward, 6 He said, "Hear now My words: If there is a prophet among you, I, the LORD, shall make Myself known to him in a vision. I shall speak with him in a dream. 7 "Not so, with My servant Moses, He is faithful in all My household; 8 With him I speak mouth to mouth, Even openly, and not in dark sayings, And he beholds the form of the LORD. Why then were you not afraid To speak against My servant, against Moses?"

The point is that, if he was greater than the prophets, Moses was surely greater than Miriam and Aaron. The way in which Moses' greater dignity is underscored is through the contrasting methods by which God appeared to him, as opposed to how He revealed Himself to the prophets. While God appeared only to the inner eyes of prophets in visions and dreams, God appeared to Moses' physical eyes in what are called theophanies.

The Apostles of Christ claimed this superior kind of contact with the resurrected Jesus. This is the force of the passages cited above. It is also clearly the force of 1 John 1:1-3 where John emphasizes physical contact with Jesus Christ.

> 1 John 1:1—What was from the beginning, what we have heard, what we have seen with our eyes, what we have looked at and touched with our hands, concerning the Word of Life. 2 And the life was manifested, and we have seen and testify and proclaim to you the eternal life, which was with the Father and was manifested to us. 3 What we have seen and heard we proclaim to you also, so that you too may have fellowship with us; and indeed our fellowship is with the Father, and with His Son Jesus Christ.

All of this emphasis on physical sight is important for this reason: visions and dreams—even if real and genuine—do not qualify one to be an Apostle of Christ. It is clear that the Bible emphasizes the distinction between the inner eye and the outer eye and counts revelation to the outer eye as a mark of superior dignity. Modern claims to have seen Jesus in a vision or dream do not qualify anyone to claim this indispensable characteristic of an Apostle of Christ.

Directly Appointed By Jesus Christ

The second indispensable characteristic of an Apostle of Christ is this: an Apostle of Christ had to be directly appointed by Jesus Christ. No church, and not even the other Apostles of Christ, were competent to select an Apostle of Christ. In strict accordance with what we have seen, only Christ can give someone His power of attorney—make someone His *sjaliach*. An Apostle of Christ must be sent—*can only be sent*—by Christ Himself. This is the reason for the explicit notice taken in two of the gospels and twice in Acts that Christ Himself chose His Apostles. This is the reason for Paul's emphatic insistence on the point that he was chosen to be an apostle by Christ Himself and not by any man or group of men.

Mark 3:14—And He appointed twelve, so that they would be with Him and that He could send them out to preach,

Luke 6:13—And when day came, He called His disciples to Him and chose twelve of them, whom He also named as apostles:

Acts 1:2—until the day when He was taken up to heaven, after He had by the Holy Spirit given orders to the apostles whom He had chosen.

Acts 10:41—not to all the people, but to witnesses who were chosen beforehand by God, that is, to us who ate and drank with Him after He arose from the dead.

Galatians 1:1—Paul, an apostle (not sent from men nor through the agency of man, but through Jesus Christ and God the Father, who raised Him from the dead).

The necessity of appointment by Christ is also the reason for the strange approach to replacing the fallen Judas Iscariot in Acts 1:24-26. Neither Peter nor the Apostles take it into their own hands to appoint a replacement. They select two men whom they knew possessed the other necessary prerequisites for an Apostle of Christ. Then they pray and cast lots in order to determine which of the two the Christ had chosen. Notice the emphasis:

Acts 1:24—And they prayed and said, "You, Lord, who know the hearts of all men, show which one of these two *You have chosen* 25 to occupy this ministry and apostleship from which Judas turned aside to go to his own place." 26 And they drew lots for them, and the lot fell to Matthias; and he was added to the eleven apostles (Emphasis mine).[9]

The Ability To Confirm His Mission By Miraculous Signs

The third indispensable characteristic of Apostles of Christ brings us directly to the subject of miracles. An Apostle of Christ was given the ability to confirm his mission by miraculous signs. The record of their calling in the Gospel of Matthew associates miracle-working with their office (Matt. 10:1-2). This is in all likelihood the implication of Acts 1:5-8 where power is promised to the eleven Apostles. Often preachers eager to apply this change to their congregation miss the clear reference to the apostles in these verses. Though there is certainly an application to the entire church in Acts 1:5-8, the fact is that the term *witnesses* designates the recipients of the promise of Acts 1:8 as the apostles. (Cf. Acts 1:22; 10:39.) The power promised includes the ability to perform miracles. The following texts show how this theme is pursued in Acts.

Acts 2:43—Everyone kept feeling a sense of awe; and many wonders and signs were taking place through the Apostles.

Acts 4:33—And with great power the Apostles were giving testimony to the resurrection of the Lord Jesus, and abundant grace was upon them all.

Acts 5:12—At the hands of the Apostles many signs and wonders were taking place among the people; and they were all with one accord in Solomon's portico.

Acts 8:14—Now when the apostles in Jerusalem heard that Samaria had received the word of God, they sent them Peter and John, 15 who came down and prayed for them that they might receive the Holy Spirit. . . . 18 Now when Simon saw that the Spirit was bestowed through the laying on of the apostles' hands, he offered them money,

Finally, this is why Paul in 2 Corinthians 12:12 can say, "The signs of a true apostle were performed among you with all perseverance, by signs and wonders and miracles." It was well known that as the direct representative of the Messiah, miraculous signs would confirm their mission. It is undeniable in light of these texts there is an important connection between the apostolate and miraculous signs.

A Further Conclusion
The evidence cited for each of these three indispensable characteristics necessitates a further conclusion. Only someone with *each* of these characteristics could claim to be an Apostle of Christ. Two out of the three were not sufficient. Every Apostle of Christ must, first, have

physically seen the resurrected Lord; second, must have been appointed directly by Christ; and, third, must have performed miraculous signs to vindicate himself as an Apostle of Christ.

In this discussion of the necessary qualifications of Apostles of Christ, we discover the first problem with many of the self-proclaimed Apostles of Christ today. If they are going to claim to be Apostles of Christ, they must possess the necessary qualifications. If someone cannot produce proof of these qualifications, they have no right to claim to be an Apostle of Christ. They also have no right to expect us to believe their claims.

The Messianic Authority Of Apostles

The Apostles of Christ were the legal representatives of Christ. They were *as the man himself.* It follows directly from this that what they said and did in their ministries as apostles Jesus said and did. This is a crucial point to understand. Consider three passages that teach this clearly.

In 1 Corinthians 14:37-38, Paul makes this point in striking terms: "If anyone thinks he is a prophet or spiritual, let him recognize that the things which I write to you are the Lord's commandment. But if anyone does not recognize this, he is not recognized." In this context Paul has been giving instructions with regard to the conduct of tongues-speakers (14:27-28), prophets (14:29-33), and women (14:33b-35) in the assemblies of the church. These were subjects that we have no record of the Lord Himself addressing while He was on earth. They are subjects about which it was very unlikely that He would have spoken while on earth, since the New Covenant church was not yet formed and the Spirit not yet given at Pentecost. In spite of this, Paul claims that what he was saying was "the Lord's commandment." This is a clear claim to speak authoritatively for the Lord Jesus Christ in apostolic office. [10]

This claim in 2 Corinthians 13:3 makes the organ of Messianic revelation explicit: "since you are seeking for proof of the Christ who speaks in me, and who is not weak toward you, but mighty in you." The reference to "the Christ who speaks in me" must not be trivialized into something that any Christian could say. It would be, in fact, an act of unspeakable daring to make such a claim. Paul refers to nothing less than the fact that the Messiah infallibly inspires what he (Paul) says in apostolic ministry.

Frequently, 1 John 4:4-6 is overlooked as an attestation of the authority of the Apostles to speak for Christ and therefore for God.

> You are from God, little children, and have overcome them; because greater is He who is in you than he who is in the world. 5 They are from the world; therefore they speak as from the world, and the world listens to them. 6 We are from God; he who knows God listens to us; he who is not from God does not listen to us. By this we know the spirit of truth and the spirit of error.

Verses four, five, and six begin, respectively, with the pronouns: you, they, and we. Some contrast is intended clearly between the "you" of verse four and both the "they" of verse five and the "we" of verse six. The contrast can be nothing else than the contrast between Christians in general in verse four, false teachers in verse five, and the Apostles of Christ in verse six. It was upon this note that the letter of 1 John began with John emphasizing the firsthand knowledge that the apostolic witnesses possessed of the Christ. There, John stresses that fellowship with God is mediated through the apostolic proclamation of this knowledge. Here John underscores that one of the marks of genuine Christianity is listening and submitting to what the Apostles of Christ proclaim. No Christian and not even any pastor ought to make the genuineness of their hearers' Christianity dependent on whether they listen to them. This is a claim only an inspired apostle can and ought to make.[11]

In very reality, one's reception of an apostle of Christ was one's reception of Christ. To reject an apostle was to forfeit Christ and His salvation.

> Matthew 10:40—He who receives you receives Me, and he who receives Me receives Him who sent Me.

> John 13:20—Truly, truly, I say to you, he who receives whomever I send receives Me; and he who receives Me receives Him who sent Me.

Again, we have here a problem for modern apostles. Those who profess to be apostles must make their being received as apostles a mark of the true Christianity of those to whom they minister. They must see themselves as clothed with the authority of Christ Himself so that if one rejects them one rejects Christ. Until they are ready to be this brave, bold, and brazen, they should cease calling themselves apostles.

But with these hints at the problem with modern apostles before us, we must now come directly to the million-dollar question: *Are there apostles today?*

1   Frederick Dale Bruner, *A Theology of the Holy Spirit* (Grand Rapids: Eerdmans, 1970), pp. 29-31, provides evidence of this as of thirty plus years ago. Nothing has happened to alter the statements he cites with regard to the worldwide importance of the renewal movements associated with Continuationism. Much has happened which underscores the worldwide spread of these movements.

2   Bruner, *A Theology of the Holy Spirit*, p.22, captures these elements of Continuationist feeling when he remarks, "There is still an additional characteristic of Pentecostal conviction which should be mentioned in any introduction to the movement: the desire for what may be called the contemporaneity of apostolic Christianity. It is important to the Pentecostal that what he reads in his New Testament be able to happen today. . . . This concern means, among other things, especially that the remarkable spiritual manifestations recorded in the New Testament such as speaking in tongues, prophecy, healing, nature miracles, and visions should continue to be experienced by Christians today."

3   Cf. for parallel uses of the beginning Acts 1:21-22; Mark 3:14.

4   Herman Ridderbos, *Redemptive History and the New Testament Scrtiptures, 2nd rev. ed.* (Phillipsburg, NJ: Presbyterian and Reformed, 1988), p. 14.

5   Ἀπόστολος

6   This is the translation of the KJV. A similar translation is given by the NKJV, ASV, and RSV.

7   John 13:16; Acts 14:4-14; Romans 16:7; 2 Cor. 8:23; and Phil. 2:25 are other possible references to small-A apostles in the New Testamant.

8   It should be noted that Acts 9:7 does not say that the men did not see the light. It says that they heard the voice, but saw no one.

9   It is to be noted that this is the only use of the lot in the New Testament after the resurrection of Christ. This extraordinary use of the lot is to be explained by the statement of Proverbs 16:33: "The lot is cast into the lap, But its every decision is from the LORD." The lot was used in Acts 1 in order to determine the decision of the Lord! Only His decision can make an Apostle of Christ. It is sometimes taught that the apostles were mistaken in selecting Matthias as the replacement for Judas. Paul, it is said, was the divinely intended replacement. From this point of view the use of the lot in this passage might also be viewed as misguided and even superstitious. The fact is, however, that Luke seems to recognize the validity of Matthias' appointment when the Spirit falls on all the apostles (Acts 2:1-4), when Peter takes his stand with the eleven other apostles (Acts 2:14, 37), when he says that the apostles generally—and not just the eleven original apostles—did miracles (Acts 2:43; 4:33), and when he refers subsequently to the twelve apostles (Acts 6:2). Also difficult for the theory that Paul should have been the replacement is the fact that James, the Lord's brother, seems also to have become an (big-A) Apostle of Christ (1 Cor. 15:7; Gal. 1:19

and cf. Gal. 2:9; Acts 12:17; 15:13; 21:18). This may have happened when the resurrected Christ appeared to him. Though the number twelve does seem to have a literal importance, this need not be pressed so strictly that we conclude that there could only have ever been twelve Apostles of Christ.

10   It is noteworthy that Paul conditions the prophetic and spiritual status of the Corinthian believers on their obedience to him. Indeed, the closing words of verse 38, "But if anyone does not recognize this, he is not recognized," may even make their being Christians depend on their obedience to His instructions (1 Cor. 8:3).

11   But it is a claim the Apostles of Christ did make and had to make. Bruner, A Theology of the Holy Spirit, p.176, is appropriately blunt when he says, "The importance, indeed the absolute importance, of the apostles as the eyewitness martures of the resurrection appearances, and of the early church to which they belonged as the sole custodian of the saving tradition of God's act in Christ, and with which, therefore, one must be in union, cannot be minimized." I think this is just the claim 1 John 1:1-3 and 4:4-6 articulate.

CHAPTER 3

THE APOSTLES: WHEN WERE THEY?

In this chapter we come to the great question regarding Apostles of Christ, which is of relevance to Continuationism: Are there Apostles of Christ today? Let me say that in asking this question I refer only to big-A Apostles of Christ. Remember the distinction established in the previous chapter.

Let me also clarify that I mean living Apostles of Christ here on earth. This may seem an obvious thing to say, since all conservative Christians agree the Apostles of Christ continue to exist in heaven. I think, however, it is important to say it. When I deny there are Apostles of Christ today, I do not want anyone to forget that the apostles continue to be the foundation of the church and continue under Christ to rule over the church from heaven through their teaching. Their teaching is the living Word of God, and it continues to have a mighty power over the church by the ongoing activity of the Spirit of Christ. Too often contemporary Christians feel at liberty to tinker with the church, as if it were under the control of their whims. They forget that it is ruled through the Apostles of Christ and the Spirit of Christ.

A further clarification is necessary. By arguing for the cessation of the apostolate, I do not mean to imply that all Continuationists disagree with this. I pointed out in the first paragraph of the Introduction that some Continuationists do believe in the cessation of the apostolate. They may not have carefully considered the implications of this, but I acknowledge that they believe it.

Are there living Apostles of Christ on earth today? I think not. I believe rather the New Testament teaches what I will call an "historically limited apostolate." That is to say, an apostolate limited to those men commissioned by Christ either shortly before (the Twelve) or shortly after (Matthias, Paul, and James, the Lord's brother) the world-redeeming events of His crucifixion and resurrection. In the rest of this chapter, we will consider the arguments for and the implications of an historically limited apostolate.

Arguments For An Historically Limited Apostolate
We will exhibit here five reasons from the Bible why there are not and cannot be Apostles of Christ on earth today. Ephesians 2:20, Matthew 16:18; and Revelation 21:14 teach that the Apostles of Christ occupy a foundational position in the church:

> Ephesians 2:20—having been built on the foundation of the apostles and prophets, Christ Jesus Himself being the corner stone,

> Matthew 16:18—"I also say to you that you are Peter, and upon this rock I will build My church; and the gates of Hades will not overpower it."

> Revelation 21:14—And the wall of the city had twelve foundation stones, and on them were the twelve names of the twelve apostles of the Lamb.

The analogy used in these texts is one of a house with foundations. The church is likened to a house that Christ will build (Note the future tense in Matt. 16:18.) during the history of the church age. This requires that an historical or chronological interpretation be given to the analogy of the foundations and superstructure of the church/house. In other words, this language suggests that the apostles are foundational in an historical sense to the universal church. Thus, they precede it in time. The foundation period of the church is, then, the first century when the original apostles lived. The superstructure period is all the following centuries of the church built on the ministry of the apostles. This restricts the Messianic apostolate to the foundational period of church history in the first century of the Christian era. Thus, it excludes the living presence in the church on earth of such apostles after the period of the church's historical founding.

THE FOUNDATION OF THE APOSTLES (EPH. 2:20)

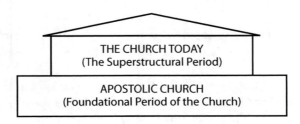

THE CHURCH TODAY
(The Superstructural Period)

APOSTOLIC CHURCH
(Foundational Period of the Church)

The Apostle Paul explicitly states that he was the last eyewitness of Christ's resurrection and the last Apostle of Christ to be appointed (1 Cor. 15:5-9).
Here are the unmistakable words of the Apostle:

> ...and that He appeared to Cephas, then to the twelve. 6 After that He appeared to more than five hundred brethren at one time, most of whom remain until now, but some have fallen asleep; 7 then He appeared to James, then to all the apostles; 8 and last of all, as to one untimely born, He appeared to me also. 9 For I am the least of the apostles, and not fit to be called an apostle, because I persecuted the church of God.

What more needs to be said? We have seen that an apostle must possess the qualification of having visibly seen the Christ in the glory of His resurrection. Since Paul says, "*last of all*, as to one untimely born, He appeared to me also," such an eyewitness of the resurrected Christ cannot be claimed today. Thus, Paul's statement in 1 Corinthians 15:9 that he was the last apostle to be chosen by Christ ought not to surprise us at all.

The Apostle Paul clearly implies that the gift of being an Apostle of Christ is no longer to be sought by Christians (1 Cor. 12:31; 14:1).[1]
In these chapters Paul encourages the Corinthians to seek the greater gifts (1 Cor. 12:31). He specifically encourages the seeking of the gift of

prophecy (1 Cor. 14:1). In spite of the fact that his list of gifts includes apostles and ranks them as the highest gift (1 Cor. 12:28 and 29), he never encourages this gift to be sought. The clear implication is that the gift of being an Apostle of Christ was no longer being given by the time of the writing of this letter.

No modern apostle is capable of receiving the commendation of the original twelve apostles, as Paul did in his day for his apostolate (Gal. 2:7-9).
In the Epistle of Galatians, Paul claims to be an apostle in the highest possible meaning of that word (Gal. 1:1, 11-17). The apostles could not have been ignorant of the claims Paul was making; yet they gave Paul the right hand of fellowship (Gal. 2:7-9).

Furthermore, Paul asserts in Galatians 2:7-9 that he was accepted by James, Cephas, and John. This was, however, in the context of the letter to the Galatians in which he made such exalted assertions regarding his apostolate (Gal. 1:1, 11-17). It would have been sheer deception to make this claim of acceptance if James, Cephas, and John were ignorant of what he was claiming.

No contemporary apostle can make the assertion of having been recognized by the original Apostles of Christ!

The final witness to the closed character of the apostolate is the closed character of the canon.
The entire Christian church acknowledges that no new book has been added to the canon of the New Testament for almost twenty centuries. There is no debate about this. Indeed, a right understanding of the nature of canonical books would not permit any new book to be added to the New Testament.[2]

Here is the reason: The New Testament gains its authority from the endorsement of the Apostles and the principle of apostolic authority. This is so, first, because the church is built on the foundation of the apostles and prophets (Eph. 2:20; Matt. 16:17), and second, because only an Apostle of Christ can claim to speak the word of Christ. It is the Apostle of Christ that is as the man himself.[3]

Since Christ is the supreme authority over the church, since Christ wrote no book, since only Apostles of Christ can speak for Christ, and since the New Testament claims authority over the church, this authority can only be grounded in apostolic authority. Thus, apostles had either to write or endorse each book of the New Testament. The fact of the closed character of the canon, therefore, assumes and implies the closed character of the apostolate.

The evidence for the historically limited apostolate presented above is cumulative. Each piece is powerful, but when taken together, it is more than adequate. It is very clear. It is, in fact, indisputable! When Cessationists build their argument against Continuationism on this evidence, they build on a solid rock indeed!

The Implications Of An Historically Limited Apostolate

There are two crucial conclusions that we must draw from the five arguments cited in the previous paragraphs of this chapter.

There is at least one gift which we know for sure cannot be possessed in the church today—the gift of being an Apostle of Christ.

This is at least one way the church today ought not to attempt to copy the church of the New Testament. When we remember that according to the New Testament being an Apostle of Christ was the first and most important gift, we can only conclude that there is a significant difference between the church of the New Testament and the church today. When we remember how crucial the apostolate was in Christ's plan for the church, and when we remember how prominent the apostolate is in the New Testament, we must conclude that there is a kind of doctrinal line or scriptural filter that separates the earliest churches from churches today. We must also consider the possibility that the cessation of the apostolate draws a doctrinal line at (or filters out) the continuation of the miraculous gifts.

Do you remember the diagram in Chapter 2? In the cessation of the apostolate we have a potential answer to the question it raises.

Is there a filter that keeps the miraculous gifts out of the church today?

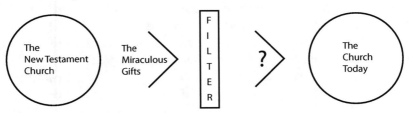

This cessation of the apostolate is indisputable. It provides a kind of doctrinal filter suggesting that the miraculous gifts do not exist in the church today. The cessation of the apostolate is, therefore, the crack in the foundation of Continuationism, the fatal flaw in their thinking. They think that to assume any distinction between the church today and the earliest church fails to take the New Testament seriously. This assumption is patently wrong.

Even Continuationists who recognize the cessation of the apostolate do not see how this should influence their thinking. It is often assumed that the presumption must be in favor of the continuation of the miraculous gifts. If, however, they admit the apostolate does not continue, why should we share this presumption?

If according to the clearest teaching of the New Testament the greatest gift is not in the church today, then surely it is possible that other gifts may also have ceased. Let me restate my point. Since we know on the clearest biblical evidence that at least one miraculous gift has ceased, this knowledge provides the crucial premise for the biblical argument for the cessation of the miraculous gifts. From this initial premise, or waterfall, a cascade of arguments thunders down against the teaching that miraculous gifts are present in today's church.

THE CASCADE ARGUMENT

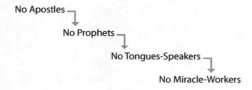

Miraculous gifts were in some measure connected with the presence of living apostles in the church.

The apostles not only performed these signs themselves, but imparted to others the ability to perform miraculous gifts (2 Cor. 12:12; Acts 8:14-20).[4] In both ways they were signs that identified the apostles as Christ's legal representatives and authenticated their message. This creates the very real possibility that with the passing of the Apostles of Christ these extraordinary gifts would also pass from the scene of the church. If this possibility is the case, then we should not expect to see the supernatural gifts in the church today. At the least this means we should not expect to see miraculous gifts to the degree that they were present in the early church. Therefore, the apostolic line that stands between the New Testament church and the church today also may prevent the extraordinary gifts present in the earliest church from now being present.

Thus, the cessation of the apostolate allows two alternative approaches to the question, Do the miraculous gifts continue? The cessation of the apostolate may indicate that there are absolutely no miraculous gifts today. It may mean that there are fewer such miraculous gifts. Either option might follow from the cessation of the apostolate. Both options make clear the difference between the apostolic church and the church today on the subject of miraculous gifts. The following outline illustrates the two options I have mentioned.

APOSTLES AND MIRACULOUS GIFTS

No Apostles ⟵┄┄⟶ No Miraculous Gifts??

No Apostles ⟵┄┄⟶ Fewer Miraculous Gifts??

In the following chapters I will argue that the cessation of the apostolate in reality means the cessation of the miraculous gifts in the church. In them we turn our attention first to the gift of prophecy.

1   This argument might appear to imply that the gift of prophecy continues even today. It seems to say that the gift of prophecy might be available, even though the gift of being an apostle is not. I agree that the argument could imply this, but I do not think that it necessarily implies this. The gift of prophecy is in a different category than the gift of being an Apostle of Christ. It might now be unavailable for reasons based on factors not present when Paul wrote 1 Corinthians and factors different than those resulting in the cessation of the apostolate and its consequently not being available when Paul wrote 1 Corinthians.

2   The claim to New Testament canonicity for any book involves the claim to be the Word of God for, and exercise rule over, the church of God. Clearly, no book outside the received canon of the New Testament can make such a claim today.

3   This paragraph raises the question of the authority and canonicity of New Testament prophets. These questions are addressed in the following chapters.

4   Douglas Judisch, *An Evaluation of Claims to the Charismatic Gifts* (Grand Rapids: Baker Book House, 1978), pp. 27-33, in a chapter entitled, "The Means of Distribution," mounts an impressive case for the thesis that "the only means of distributing the prophetic gifts in the New Testament era was the apostolate, so that once the last apostle died, no more prophetic gifts were available." (33) Though my argument in no way depends on this thesis, the case that Judisch mounts for it should not be lightly dismissed. Even if the reader finally concludes that his careful examination of Acts 8, 1 Corinthians 12:12, and Hebrews 2:3-4 falls short of an airtight proof for his thesis, his interpretation of these key passages deserves study and certainly shows that an important link existed between the Apostles of Christ and the Charismatic gifts. At any rate, it is difficult to explain the events of Acts 8 without the thesis that the Apostles of Christ alone distributed the extraordinary gifts of the Spirit. It seems very clear that the major—if not the exclusive—means of their distribution to the church was through the Apostles of Christ.

PART 2

PROPHETS

CHAPTER 4

OLD TESTAMENT PROPHETS

INTRODUCTION

When I originally developed the critique of Continuationism now presented in this book, I was teaching it in the adult Sunday School class in my church. I think I shocked my students when I introduced the study on the gift of prophets and prophecy in this way:

> I have something very shocking to say to you. I can prove to you that there is prophecy in the church today! I can prove it to you very simply. According to the Bibles you hold in your hands, and in particular Revelation 1:1-3, the book of Revelation is a prophecy. We are a church. There is, thus, prophecy in the church today. Any questions?

I began that way partly, I suppose, to get their attention. I was also making the point that the question before us was not whether there is prophetic revelation in the church today. We agree most heartily with every Charismatic and Continuationist that there is. The question is whether there are *living* prophets of Christ in the church today. This is a different question. It is very important that we distinguish these two things. This distinction will become important in this study of biblical prophets.

In this study of the gift of prophets we are concerned in particular with New Testament prophets and prophecy. I want to begin by acknowledging that this is a different and more difficult issue than the question of New Testament apostles. True, our study of the Apostles of Christ has given us an important precedent. We now know that one gift, and the most important gift, —the gift of being an Apostle of Christ—no longer has living representatives in the church. This makes it plausible to argue that living prophets no longer inhabit the church on earth. This perspective must not be viewed as some sort of strange or alien idea that has only recently infiltrated an unsuspecting Christian world. The truth is that this view has deep historical roots in the church.

Yet it seems to me we must build on the foundation already laid and say more about the cessation of the prophetic gift. I have argued that prophets were secondary to Apostles of Christ. I have also argued that, while in 1 Corinthians Paul regarded the apostolate as closed, he urged Christians to seek the gift of prophecy. Might this imply that Christians today should seek the gift of prophecy? As we have seen, it is popular in our day to admit that the apostolate is closed, but to argue that a kind of prophet continues in the church.[1] Is it possible, though there are no longer living apostles, there may be living prophets? This is the question that we must address.

To answer, we must not begin with the New Testament prophets. They were not the original, biblical prophets. Long before prophets arose in the New Testament church, prophets were recognized and regulated in the Old Testament. Failure to begin with the Old Testament prophets in this discussion is akin to a history of the Roman Empire that ignores the previous five hundred year existence of the Roman Republic. It is like attempting to study World War II with no reference to World War I. Even more cogently, it would be like trying to understand the offices and work of Christ without the aid of the Old Testament. New Testament prophecy arose within a Jewish community whose acquaintance with prophecy was overshadowed by the giant figures of the Old Testament prophets. We must, therefore, begin with the institution of Old Testament prophecy.

Let me add a word of personal testimony. It has been a major help to me in coming to clear views with regard to the claims of Continuationists to have studied and taught for many years a course in the *Doctrine of the Word*. Teaching this course forced me to grapple with the identity of Old Testament prophecy and its importance in the formation of the Old Testament. It delivered me from the superficial view of prophecy that, I believe, facilitates most Continuationism. This is the reason why the present chapter is dedicated to providing the reader with a clear understanding of the nature and importance of Old Testament prophets. If the material does not seem immediately relevant, please give me the benefit of the doubt. I think you will see its importance as we come to the following two chapters on the subject of New Testament prophecy.

THE OLD TESTAMENT PROPHETS

The Identity of Old Testament Prophecy

The first and most basic question that may be asked about prophecy is, "What is a prophet?" A pair of parallel passages, and a pair of parallel names, will help answer this question.

The parallel passages are Exodus 4:10-17 and 7:1-2. Together these passages teach us that a prophet was the mouth or spokesman of God:

> Then Moses said to the LORD, "Please, Lord, I have never been eloquent, neither recently nor in time past, nor since You have spoken to Your servant; for I am slow of speech and slow of tongue." 11 The LORD said to him, "Who has made man's mouth? Or who makes him mute or deaf, or seeing or blind? Is it not I, the LORD? 12 "Now then go, and I, even I, will be with your mouth, and teach you what you are to say." 13 But he said, "Please, Lord, now send the message by whomever You will." 14 Then the anger of the LORD burned against Moses, and He said, "Is there not your brother Aaron the Levite? I know that he speaks fluently. And moreover, behold, he is coming out to meet you; when he sees you, he will be glad in his heart. 15 "You are to speak to him and put the words in his mouth; and I, even I, will be with your mouth and his mouth, and I will teach you what you are to do. 16 "Moreover, he shall speak for you to the people; and he will be as a mouth for you and you will be as God to him. 17 "You shall take in your hand this staff, with which you shall perform the signs." Then the LORD said to Moses, "See, I make you as God to Pharaoh, and your brother Aaron shall be your prophet. 2 "You shall speak all that I command you, and your brother Aaron shall speak to Pharaoh that he let the sons of Israel go out of his land.

The LORD's words to Moses in Exodus 7:1-2 make clear that the prophet was one who spoke for God. He was, in other words, and as Exodus 4:10-17 shows, *the mouth of God.*

The parallel names are "prophet" and "seer." These two names were basically synonymous (1 Sam. 9:9; Isa. 30:9, 10). They do emphasize, however, different aspects of what it means to be a prophet. The name seer stresses the method of receiving revelations, which characterized the prophetic institution. These men saw *visions* (Numbers 12:1-8). The name "prophet" and the related verb "to prophesy" stresses that a prophet is a divine spokesman or a spokesman for God. B. B. Warfield says:

> The fundamental passage which brings the central fact before us in the most vivid manner is, no doubt, the account of the commissioning of Moses and Aaron given in Ex. iv. 10-17; vii. 1-7. Here, in the most express words, Jehovah declares that He who made the mouth can be with it to teach it what to speak, and announces the precise function of a prophet to be that he is "a mouth of God," who speaks not his own but God's words. Accordingly, the Hebrew name for "prophet" (nabhi'), whatever may be its etymology, means throughout the Scriptures just "spokesman," though not "spokesman" in general, but spokesman by way of eminence, that is, God's spokesman; and the characteristic formula by which a prophetic declaration is announced is: "The word of Jehovah came to me," or the brief "saith Jehovah".[2]

It is, therefore, legitimate to say that the term "prophet" stresses the prophet's relation to the people. He speaks to them God's Word. "Seer," on the other hand, stresses his relation to God. He receives visions from God. *Seer* stresses the reception of the message. Prophet stresses the deliverance of a message.

The Regulation of Old Testament Prophecy

It is not surprising that an institution that embodied the very words of God would be the subject of careful instruction and regulation by God. Old Testament prophecy is further defined and regulated in two crucial passages in Deuteronomy. Deuteronomy 13:1-5 is the first passage.

> If a prophet or a dreamer of dreams arises among you and gives you a sign or a wonder, 2 and the sign or the wonder comes true, concerning which he spoke to you, saying, 'Let us go after other gods (whom you have not known) and let us serve them,' 3 you shall not

listen to the words of that prophet or that dreamer of dreams; for the LORD your God is testing you to find out if you love the LORD your God with all your heart and with all your soul. 4 "You shall follow the LORD your God and fear Him; and you shall keep His commandments, listen to His voice, serve Him, and cling to Him. 5 "But that prophet or that dreamer of dreams shall be put to death, because he has counseled rebellion against the LORD your God who brought you from the land of Egypt and redeemed you from the house of slavery, to seduce you from the way in which the LORD your God commanded you to walk. So you shall purge the evil from among you.

A number of matters with regard to prophecy become clear in this passage. It assumes, for instance, that a prophet attested his message by some sign or wonder. It teaches, even if a supposed prophet attested himself by some such wonder, his message was not to be followed or believed if he led the people away from the revelation of the true God that had been given to them by Moses. The solemnity of making a claim to be a prophet is underscored by the punishment for a false prophet. Such a prophet was to be executed.

Deuteronomy 18:15-22 is the second passage:

"The LORD your God will raise up for you a prophet like me from among you, from your countrymen, you shall listen to him. 16 "This is according to all that you asked of the LORD your God in Horeb on the day of the assembly, saying, 'Let me not hear again the voice of the LORD my God, let me not see this great fire anymore, or I will die.' 17 "The LORD said to me, 'They have spoken well. 18 'I will raise up a prophet from among their countrymen like you, and I will put My words in his mouth, and he shall speak to them all that I command him. 19 'It shall come about that whoever will not listen to My words which he shall speak in My name, I Myself will require it of him. 20 'But the prophet who speaks a word presumptuously in My name which I have not commanded him to speak, or which he speaks in the name of other gods, that prophet shall die.' 21 "You may say in your heart, 'How will we know the word which the LORD has not spoken?' 22 "When a prophet speaks in the name of the LORD, if the thing does not come about or come true, that is the thing which the LORD has not spoken. The prophet has spoken it presumptuously; you shall not be afraid of him.

If it is to be understood properly, several crucial observations on this passage will be helpful:

Though this passage has a fulfillment in Christ as the great and final prophet, it also refers to the line of prophets that arose in the Theocracy of Israel (Acts 3:17-26). These two (seemingly contradictory) fulfillments of the passage are consistent because it was the Spirit of Christ who spoke in the prophets of the Old Testament (1 Peter 1:11).

It is clear from this passage, though Moses was more than a prophet; he was also a prophet (vv. 15-18). Moses is described as a prophet, because he was the mouth or spokesman of God. Moses is contrasted with the prophets, because God spoke to him face to face and not merely through dreams and visions—the characteristic way in which prophets received their revelations (Num. 12:18).

It is clear that a prophet is a spokesman for God into whose mouth God puts His own words (v. 18). The fact that God puts His words into the very mouth of the prophet becomes quite significant as an argument against contemporary Continuationism.

It is clear that God's prophets spoke with divine authority (vv. 19-21). The prophet's words are the words spoken by the Lord (v. 21). They are, says Jehovah, "My words in his mouth" (v. 18). Thus, not listening to the true prophet was a sin for which God would exact punishment (v. 19).[3]

It is clear that false prophets were to be punished with the death penalty (v. 20). Again, this underscores the dignity and solemnity of the prophetic office and, by implication, any claim to be a prophet.

It is clear that one definitive mark of a false prophet is that something he speaks in the name of the Lord does not come true (vv. 21-22). One mistaken prophecy was sufficient to reveal that a professed prophet was a false prophet.

Putting these two passages together, we can say a true prophet possesses, and must possess, two infallible marks. First, what he prophesies must *always* come true. Second, he must not contradict previous revelation, but teach people to follow the true God (the God revealed through Moses).

The Varieties of Old Testament Prophecy

What has been said already indicates we must distinguish nuances of meaning within the biblical idea of prophecy. Every true prophet most basically is the spokesman or mouth of God. As we have seen, even

Moses is in this sense a prophet (Deut. 18:15-22). Yet, the characteristic media by which revelation was given to a prophet are indicated by the designation seer. A prophet characteristically received his revelations by means of dreams and visions (Num. 12:1-8). Since Moses did not characteristically receive the revelation given him through the media of visions and dreams, in this sense he may be distinguished from the prophets.

Another shade of meaning in the idea of Old Testament prophecy may also be isolated. Sometimes the prophets are specifically those messengers of God sent to Theocratic Israel pursuant to the ministry of Moses. Thus, Acts 3:24 reads, "And likewise, all the prophets who have spoken, from Samuel and *his* successors onward, also announced these days." Here the prophetic line appears to begin with Samuel and the reference seems to be to the Theocratic prophets. Though Moses and Abel (Luke 11:51) were prophets in the broader sense of being spokemen for God, they were not Theocratic prophets in the sense that Samuel was. The following diagram seeks to illustrate the nuances or shades of meaning in the idea of Old Testament prophecy from the most basic or foundational meanings to the more narrow.

OLD TESTAMENT PROPHECY

AN INSTITUTION
Theocratic Messengers to Israel
Abel was not a prophet in this sense (Luke 11:51)
Moses was not a prophet in this sense (Acts 3:24)

A MODE
Seers of Visions
Moses was more than a prophet in this sense (Num 12:6-8)

A FUNCTION
Spokesman for God
Moses was a propeht in this basic sense (Deut 18:15, 18)

Again, the relevance of all this may not be immediately evident. It will, however, become evident when we come to consider Continuationist perspectives on New Testament prophecy.

The Authority of Old Testament Prophecy

The divine authority of Old Testament prophecy has already been vindicated. What could be clearer? The prophet is the spokesman, the very mouth of God. God says that his words are "My words in his mouth." Those who do not listen to the prophet are punished by God. Several questions are raised that tend to cast doubt on the divine authority of the prophets. It is necessary to answer these questions so that no doubt remains with reference to the absolute authority of the prophetic message.

Does the superiority of Moses to the prophets imply the inferior authority of their message (Num. 12:1-8)? No. There is no contrast at this point. It is the comparative clarity and dignity of Moses relative to the prophets that is emphasized, not his comparative authority. The New Testament is superior to the Old Testament (2 Cor. 3:1-18; Heb. 1:1-2a), but this does not mean that it is more inspired, infallible, or inerrant. Warfield helpfully observes:

> But though Moses was thus distinguished above all others in the dealings of God with him, no distinction is drawn between the revelations given through him and those given through other organs of revelation in point either of Divinity or of authority. And beyond this we have no Scriptural warrant to go in contrasting one mode of revelation with another .... In whatever diversity of forms, by means of whatever variety of modes, in whatever distinguishable stages it is given, it is ever the revelation of the One God, and it is ever the one consistently developing redemptive revelation of God.[4]

Does the identification of prophecy with the media of dreams and visions imply that the prophets were left to their own powers in communicating the message received? No. The prophetic mode of revelation involves both the reception and deliverance of the message. The one given prophecy is called both a seer and a prophet. The first word emphasized the receiving, the second the delivering of the message (Deut. 18:18-22; Exod. 4:10-17). Many passages emphasize the infallible utterance of the message by the true prophet (Jer. 1:9, 5:14; Isa. 51:16; Num. 22:35; 23:5, 12, 16; Ezek. 3:4). 2 Peter 1:19-21 is particularly important in its description of how "men moved by the Holy Spirit spoke from God." Warfield's comments helpfully elucidate the meaning of the key word, *moved*:

The term here used is a very specific one. It is not to be confounded with guiding, or directing, or controlling, or even leading in the full sense of that word. It goes beyond all such terms, in assigning the effect produced specifically to the active agent. What is "borne" is taken up by the "bearer," and conveyed by the "bearer's" power, not its own, to the "bearer's" goal, not its own. The men who spoke from God are here declared, therefore, to have been taken up by the Holy Spirit and brought by His power to the goal of His choosing. The things which they spoke under this operation of the Spirit were therefore His things, not theirs.[5]

Does the fact that the prophetic mode of revelation involves both the reception and delivery of a message imply a mechanical control of the prophet and suspension of his humanity? No. God's control of the prophet is intimately organic, not externally mechanical. God accommodated the prophet to the prophecy, before accommodating the prophecy to the prophet. That is to say, God uses His instruments in accordance with their natures and forms those natures with his purposes in mind. Therefore, it is no contradiction of the full divinity and authority of the prophetic word that it is permeated with the marks of Isaiah's or Amos' personality.

The Canonicity of Old Testament Prophecy

Just as the books written or endorsed by the Apostles of Christ were for that very reason the canon of the New Testament, so also the writings of Moses and the prophets were for that very reason the canon of the Old Testament. This is what I mean by their canonicity. The canon of the Old Testament was twofold. It was composed of Moses (or the law) and the prophets. Prophetic writings were by nature, therefore, canonical writings.[6] Several considerations confirm these assertions.

This is why the Old Testament canon was closed when the "spirit of prophecy" departed from Israel after Haggai, Zechariah, and Malachi—the last Old Testament prophets before the coming of John the Baptist. The Jews that lived between the Old and New Testament periods recognized there were no longer any prophets. R. Laird Harris cites four witnesses:

That this was the view of the inter-Testamental period is witnessed not only by I Maccabees, in which the defiled stones of the Temple are commanded to be put aside "until a prophet should arise" (I Macc. 4:46; cf. 9:27; 14:41), but also now by the Dead Sea manual of Discipline, which looks forward to the time of the "coming of a Prophet and the anointed ones of Aaron and Israel." In the meantime, the Torah and the previously mentioned words of the prophets and the rule of the community shall obtain. Much the same idea is expressed somewhat later by the statements of Josephus, who declared that "the prophets wrote from the days of Moses to Artaxerxes very particularly but that later writers hath not been esteemed of the like authority with the former by our forefathers, because there hath not been an exact succession of prophets since that time." Similar is the Talmudic reference, "After the latter prophets Haggai, Zechariah, and Malachi, the Holy Spirit departed from Israel."[7]

The New Testament and the writings of the Judaism that existed in the period between the Old and New Testaments point to the prophetic institution as the sole source of Old Testament Scripture after Moses. Here are some of the most important facts: (1) Inter-Testamental Judaism, as we have just seen, seems to have regarded all of the books outside the law as prophetic. (2) The New Testament normally designates the Old Testament as having two parts: the law (or Moses) and the prophets (Matt. 5:17; 7:12; 11:13; Luke 16:16; John. 1:45; Acts 13:15; 24:14; 28:23; Rom. 3:21; Luke 16:29, 31; 24:27; Acts 26:22). (3) Sometimes the New Testament designates the entire Old Testament simply as the prophets even when a writing of Moses or the Psalms is in view (Matt. 26:56; Luke 1:70f. [Note the quotation of the Psalms.]; Luke 18:31; 24:25f; Acts 2:30; 3:21; 7:52; [There is a possible reference to Moses here.] 2 Peter 1:19-21).

There is also the explicit testimony of the Old Testament that most of its books were, in fact, written by prophets. There is no evidence that any of the books were written by anyone who was not at least in the broad sense noted earlier a prophet. Though the Psalms and Daniel are traditionally classed in a third category called the *Writings*, there is biblical testimony that both Daniel (Matt. 24:15) and authors of the Psalms—David (Acts 2:30) and Asaph (2 Chron. 29:30)—were prophets.

The only possible biblical testimony to this threefold division is Luke 24:44 where the reference is to the "law of Moses, and . . . the prophets, and . . . the Psalms." Several things show that this reference does not prove a threefold classification of the Old Testament. (1) The passage does not mention the *Writings*, only the Psalms. (2) This single reference must be contrasted with the normal New Testament twofold division of the Old Testament into the law (or Moses) and the prophets. (3) It must also be seen in light of the places noted above where the New Testament describes the entire Old Testament as prophetic. (4) It must also be weighed against the acknowledged prophetic status of several of the authors of the Psalms. When these contrasts are weighed, there is little reason to think that this single reference is proof of a threefold division of the Old Testament. The Psalms may be singled out in Luke 24:44 because of their distinctive character as hymns or psalms or because the Psalms are peculiarly prophetic of Christ and His work.

In this chapter we have considered the identity, regulation, varieties, authority, and canonicity of Old Testament prophecy. With this solid foundation under our feet, we are now in a position to consider the claims of Continuationism about New Testament prophecy and its existence in the church today.

1   Wayne A. Grudem, *Systematic Theology,* pp.1031-1061.

2   B. B. Warfield, *Revelation and Inspiration* [in vol. 1 of the Works of Benjamin
    B. Warfield] (Grand Rapids: Baker Book House, 1981), p.19.

3   According to Acts 3:22-23, not heeding the words of the true prophet would
    result in being "utterly destroyed from among the people."

4   Warfield, *Revelation and Inspiration,* pp.15-16.

5   Op. cit., p.83.

6   The reader may wonder about those prophetic writings that were not pre-
    served. Does the fact that some prophetic writings were not preserved and
    so are not part of the canon of the church today mean that they were not ca-
    nonical? Does the fact that those writings were not preserved argue against
    their canonicity? Canonicity, it must be remembered, derives from the divine
    authority of a writing. If God gives a prophetic message to His people, it is
    necessarily part of the rule of canon of the people of God. The canon is the
    rule, standard, or authority of God's people. Simply because God did not see fit
    to include by His preserving providence a prophetic writing in the permanent
    canon of the people of God, does not mean that it was not canonical for that
    part of the people of God who received it and for as long as they had it. Just as
    the principle of New Testament authority is apostolic, so the principle of Old
    Testament authority is (Mosaic and) prophetic. The fact that a given apostolic
    writing (such as the missing epistle of Paul to the Corinthians) was not pre-
    served does not argue against the principle of apostolic authority. It only tells
    us that Providence, for reasons of its own, did not see fit to preserve it to be part
    of the continuing and universal standard of the church. Because of the prin-
    ciple of apostolic authority, it would necessarily have been canonical, if it had
    been preserved. Even so, the principle of prophetic authority is not diminished
    if certain of their utterances or sayings are not preserved. Because whatever
    a prophet said as a prophet was authoritative, the utterance would have been
    authoritative and in that sense canonical for Israel had it been preserved.

7   R. Laird Harris, *The Inspiration and Canonicity of the Bible* (Grand Rapids:
    Zondervan, 1957), p. 169.

CHAPTER 5

NEW TESTAMENT PROPHETS

ARGUMENTS FOR THEIR CONTINUATION

We shall spend, as already mentioned, this chapter and the next considering New Testament prophets and prophecy. In this chapter we will consider the arguments brought forward by Continuationists for the continuation of New Testament prophets in the church today. In the next we will consider the arguments for their cessation.

New Testament prophecy was given for purposes not yet fulfilled.
Ephesians 4:11-13 mentions a number of purposes which New Testament prophecy was given to achieve.

> And He gave some as apostles, and some as prophets, and some as evangelists, and some as pastors and teachers, 12 for the equipping of the saints for the work of service, to the building up of the body of Christ; 13 until we all attain to the unity of the faith, and of the knowledge of the Son of God, to a mature man, to the measure of the stature which belongs to the fullness of Christ.

Charismatics and Continuationists note that prophets (as well as the other gifts mentioned in Eph. 4:11-13) were given to bring the church "to the measure of the stature of the fullness of Christ" (v. 13). They proceed to argue that, since this goal has clearly not been reached, this passage strongly suggests New Testament prophecy continues. Several problems with this use of the passage become evident when it is more carefully considered.

This interpretation requires (since apostles are also mentioned) that there be Apostles of Christ in the church today. In other words, Apostles of Christ were also given to bring the church "to the measure of the stature of the fullness of Christ" (v. 13). Thus, this interpretation leads to the conclusion not only that the prophets mentioned continue, but that the Apostles of Christ continue. We have seen that there are cogent reasons to reject this idea. Indeed, most Continuationists also reject this notion. Thus, this interpretation proves too much. Since it proves something we know is wrong, the interpretation itself cannot be correct.

This interpretation forgets that the ministry of both the apostles and the prophets did not cease with their death. The church continues to be ministered unto by the writings of apostles and prophets. In the previous chapter, I showed that there is clearly prophecy (in written form) in the church today from Revelation 1:1-3. In this way, prophecy does continue in the church today, but this does not mean *living* prophets remain in the church.

New Testament prophecy ceases only with the Second Coming of Christ.

1 Corinthians 13:8-13 is used by Continuationists in a way similar to Ephesians 4:11-13. This passage seems, however, even more supportive of their view. The key verse is verse ten:

> Love never fails; but if there are gifts of prophecy, they will be done away; if there are tongues, they will cease; if there is knowledge, it will be done away. 9 For we know in part and we prophesy in part; 10 but when the perfect comes, the partial will be done away. 11 When I was a child, I used to speak like a child, think like a child, reason like a child; when I became a man, I did away with childish things. 12 For now we see in a mirror dimly, but then face to face; now I know in part, but then I will know fully just as I also have been fully known. 13 But now faith, hope, love, abide these three; but the greatest of these is love (Emphasis mine).

Several comments will make the Continuationist argument clear to those unfamiliar with it.

Continuationists equate *the partial* of verse ten with the gifts of prophecy and tongues mentioned in the previous verses. In other words, "the partial which will be done away" refers to the gifts of prophecy and tongues mentioned in verses eight and nine.

They argue that *the perfect* is the condition ushered in by the Second Coming of Christ.

They stress that the verse asserts that the partial is done away with *when* the perfect comes.

They, therefore, conclude that tongues and prophecy are by this passage clearly declared to continue until the Second Coming of Christ. *If* only when the perfect comes, is the partial done away, *then* prophecy and tongues obviously continue until the perfect condition ushered in by the Second Coming of Christ.

This passage so interpreted does certainly provide an impressive argument for the continuation of the gifts of prophecy and tongues. This argument deserves to be carefully addressed.

Not a few Cessationists have attempted to defeat this argument by denying that the perfect is the condition ushered in by the Second Coming of Christ.[1] They argue instead that the perfect is the condition ushered in by the completion of the canon. Though I esteem those of my fellow Cessationists who hold this view, I cannot accept their arguments. It seems clear to me that verse ten and verse twelve are parallel: "For now we see in a mirror dimly, but then face to face; now I know in part, but then I will know fully just as I also have been fully known." To me, verse twelve seems clearly to refer to the condition of the eternal state ushered in by Christ's Second Coming (2 Cor. 5:7; 1 John 3:2).[2] On this point of interpretation I agree with the Continuationists.

The flaw in the Continuationist use of these verses is to be found elsewhere. It is to be found, I am convinced, in the way their interpretation equates *the partial* of verse ten with the gifts of tongues and prophecy. If this loose thread is pulled, it will unravel the Continuationist argument.

Verse eight does not speak of prophecy singular, but of prophecies *plural.*[3] The emphasis, therefore, is not on the gift of prophecy *itself,* but on the various revelations or *prophecies* given through the gift. Thus, verse eight emphasizes not the gift of prophecy, but the contents of prophecy—the *prophecies* plural given through the gift of prophecy.

The emphasis, then, of the preceding context is not on the gifts of tongues and prophecy. It is clearly on the knowledge—the partial knowledge—associated with those gifts. Verse nine does after all say, "For we know in part and we prophesy in part."[4] This statement emphasizes the partial character of the knowledge conveyed *through* the gift of prophecy.

Though there is a contrast between the partial and the perfect in verse nine, this contrast means there is also a parallel between them. If the partial refers to the partial gift, then by analogy the perfect must refer to the perfect gift. But what sense would this way of reading the verse make? Of course, the Continuationists do not think that the perfect in verse ten refers to the perfect gift. But that is just my point. Since the Continuationist thinks the partial refers to the partial gifts of prophecy and tongues, *by analogy and because of the parallel* the perfect on his reading must refer to some perfect gift. This reading of the passage is, however, nonsense—as even Continuationists recognize. What would the perfect gift mean?

The nonsense in which such a reading results confirms the interpretation that the partial is not the partial gift, but the partial knowledge. *The contrast is between the partial knowledge of the present state and the perfect knowledge of the eternal state.*

This is confirmed by the emphasis of verse twelve on perfect knowledge: "For now we see in a mirror dimly, but then face to face; now I know in part, but then I will know fully just as I also have been fully known."

Our present partial knowledge was communicated through the gifts of prophecy and tongues. The future perfect knowledge will be communicated through the Second Coming of Christ. Thus, the analogy and parallel between the perfect and the partial in verse ten leads surely to the conclusion that the partial is not a reference to the gifts of prophecy and tongues, but the partial knowledge imparted through them.

The conclusion must be that Paul is teaching the doing away of partial knowledge in favor of perfect knowledge in verse ten. He says nothing about when the gifts of prophecy and tongues pass away. He only refers to the passing of the present partial knowledge that was conveyed through those gifts. He leaves open the question of the time of the passing of the gifts of prophecy and tongues.[5] This passage is, therefore, not conclusive for the continuation of the gift of prophecy. That issue must be decided on other grounds.[6]

The bottom line is that the argument for Continuationism from 1 Corinthians 13:10 is inconclusive. This does not bother Cessationists who need not build their case on this passage and who support their position on other grounds. It does, however, substantially weaken the Continuationist view by destabilizing one of its main supports.

New Testament prophecy is significantly different from Old Testament prophecy.

With the increasing prevalence of the Charismatic and Pentecostal movements in the last century, the meaning of prophecy in the New Covenant has taken on a fresh importance. One familiar with the Puritans will have noticed that they often assumed that prophesying was generally equivalent to what we call preaching. (Note *The Art of Prophesying* by William Perkins.) On the other hand, Continuationists have attempted to distance New Testament prophecy from Old Testament prophecy in order to deliver it from having to meet the strict standards laid down for Old Testament prophecy in Deuteronomy 18. This is the position of the well-known Continuationist, Wayne Grudem.[7] The question, therefore, must be squarely faced. Is it possible to distinguish New Testament prophecy from Old Testament prophecy in such a way as to allow for something less than infallibility in its deliverances? The rest of this chapter will be dedicated to proving two assertions that require a negative answer.

The Bible never explicitly or overtly distinguishes New Testament prophecy from Old Testament prophecy.

New Testament prophets are never explicitly or overtly distinguished from Old Testament prophets. This is the simple fact of the matter, and it is a fact by itself conclusive for the question at hand. We must not forget that, when prophecy and prophets are mentioned in the church after Pentecost, these words and the institution they represented were well known to the Jews. Old Testament prophecy was, by common consent, inspired and infallible in its pronouncements (Deut. 18:15-22). If New Testament prophecy in distinction from Old Testament prophecy was not infallible in its pronouncements, this would have constituted an absolutely fundamental contrast between the Old Testament institution and the New Testament institution. To suppose that a difference as important as this would be passed over without explicit comment is unthinkable.

Continuationists have attempted to present evidence from the Bible for such a distinction for New Testament prophecy. They have cited various biblical data to make their case, but the arguments they propose do not approach the kind of explicit precedent the situation requires. There is certainly no overt testimony to such a distinction as they wish.

They attempt to *imply* the fallibility of New Testament prophecy by showing that it was to be evaluated (1 Cor. 14:29; 1 Thess. 5:19-21) on the basis of Scripture. The problem is Old Testament prophecy was also evaluated on the basis of Scripture (previous revelation). Deuteronomy 13:1-5 makes this patent. Clearly, this fact did not mean true, Old Testament prophecy was less than infallible.

Similarly, Continuationists note that the prophets were subordinate to the Apostles of Christ. This is said in order to *imply* their fallibility. It is certainly true that the New Testament prophets were inferior in rank to the Apostles. This is suggested, for instance, by the consistent New Testament order in which apostles are mentioned first and prophets second (1 Cor. 12:29; Eph. 2:20; 3:5; 4:11). This subordinate position does not, however, imply their fallibility. As we have seen, the Old Testament prophets were distinctly inferior to Moses in the place they held in the nation of Israel (Num. 12:1-8). This, however, did not imply their fallibility.

It may be argued that the New Testament prophets were of a different order than the Theocratic prophets designated by the phrase, "Samuel and all the prophets" (Acts 3:24; 13:20; Heb. 11:32). But then so also were Abel, Enoch, Moses, and Jesus—all of whom the Bible describes as infallible prophets (Luke 11:51; Jude 1:14; Acts 3:20-23). Not just the Theocratic prophets, but all other true, biblical prophets were regarded as infallible in their pronouncements. Indeed, as we have seen, such infallibility was basic, indispensable, and necessary to being a true prophet (Deut. 18:15-22).

Continuationists argue that Agabus (whom all must admit was a New Testament prophet) erred in his prophecy regarding Paul in Acts 21:10-11.[8]

> As we were staying there for some days, a prophet named Agabus came down from Judea. 11 And coming to us, he took Paul's belt and bound his own feet and hands, and said, "This is what the Holy Spirit says: 'In this way the Jews at Jerusalem will bind the man who owns this belt and deliver him into the hands of the Gentiles.'"

This is an amazing—not to say shocking—claim. If it were true, however, it would certainly be a significant piece of information. A number of responses may be made to this claim that conclusively show it is wrong.

Only by applying the most wooden and stringent principles of interpretation to the prophecy of Agabus are Continuationists able to suggest the prophecy of Agabus was tinged with error. Gaffin argues against such an interpretation of Agabus by saying, "In general, this attempt suffers from the demand for pedantic precision imposed on Agabus."[9] A simple reading of the prophecy shows, in fact, what Agabus predicted actually and literally happened.[10] It is to be feared that the interpretive approach used by Continuationists with reference to Agabus, if applied to the to the rest of the Bible, would uncover errors in many places where conservative Continuationists would not like to find them.

More importantly, neither Luke nor the rest of the Bible adversely criticizes Agabus' prophecy.[11] Nowhere do we find Luke or any other author of Scripture finding fault with Agabus' predictions.

The view that tinges Agabus' prophecy with error neglects the important interpretive principle of the author's intention in recording these events. We must ask, in other words, why Luke included the prophecy of Agabus in his narrative. What was his intention in recording this prophecy? Did it have anything to do with teaching us the fallibility of Agabus? When we ask this question and examine Acts for an answer, it becomes clear Luke is developing the theme of Paul's courage in the face of the certain persecution that awaited him in Jerusalem. Agabus has already been identified as a true prophet in Acts 11:28, where it is explicitly stated that his prophecy of famine in Jerusalem came to pass. In Acts 20:23, Paul is quoted as saying that "the Holy Spirit solemnly testifies to me in every city, saying that bonds and afflictions await me."[12] In Acts 28:17, Paul refers to what happened to him in Jerusalem in language reminiscent of the details of Agabus' prophecy.[13] To introduce the idea that Agabus erred into this theme is to ignore and to undo the authorial intention of Luke.[14]

Continuationists argue that contemporary prophets receive a revelation or vision from God, but are not preserved from garbling the message when they utter it. Strictly speaking, this would mean they are seers and not prophets, a distinction nowhere made in the Bible. It would also mean they are false prophets (Deut. 18:15-22). Nowhere does the Bible make a provision for a well-meaning seer who garbles his message.

None of the attempts to find a distinction between Old and New Testament prophecy are viable. It is undeniable that the key distinction at which the defender of Continuationism is aiming is simply absent from the New Testament.

The New Testament in many ways encourages us to equate the authority of Old and New Testament prophecy.

The authority of Old and New Testament prophecy is equated by many features of the New Testament:

In the first place, there is no terminological distinction between Old and New Testament prophecy. The identical terms are used to describe both in the New Testament.

In the second place, indiscriminate references to Old and New Testament prophecy using this identical terminology lie side by side repeatedly in the Acts. For example, Old Testament prophets and prophecy are mentioned in Acts 2:16; 3:24, 25; 10:43; 13:27, 40; 15:15; 24:14; 26:22, 27; and 28:23. References to New Testament prophets and prophecy are interspersed without comment or distinction (Acts 2:17-18; 7:37; 11:27, 28; 13:1; 15:32; 21:9-11).

In the third place, the pivotal prophecy (Acts 2:16-21) clearly equates Old and New Testament prophecy. It tells us that the Old Testament *prophet* Joel prophesied in the Old Testament that in the New Covenant "your sons and daughters shall prophesy" with young men seeing visions and old men having dreams. The Continuationist distinction between Old and New Testament prophecy is clearly obliterated here.

In the fourth place, the book of Revelation is described as a prophecy. Plainly, it is a New Testament prophecy. Its prophetic status, however, assures its infallibility as written and brings down upon its violators the divine curse (Rev. 1:3; 22:7, 10, 18, 19).

In the fifth place, the emphasis of the New Testament is that the New Covenant is a better covenant and superior to the Old (Hebrews 8:1-13; 2 Cor. 3:1-6). This places in a strange light the Continuationist contention that New Testament prophecy is, in the most significant respect, inferior to the Old.

In the sixth place, we must not forget that the New Testament prophet *par excellence* is the Lord Jesus Christ Himself. Acts 3:22-23 emphasizes that whatever He speaks is to be obeyed. His words, therefore, are infallible. Continuationists may argue that it is unfair to bring up the example of the Lord Jesus. They might contend the

Messiah's pronouncements are infallible and that there is no comparison between the Messiah and other New Testament prophets. This cannot disguise the fact, however, that Jesus was a New Testament prophet and that He was infallible. This does nothing to encourage the thesis that New Testament prophecy is inferior in point of infallibility to that of the Old Testament.

CONCLUSIONS

Three crucial conclusions must be drawn from the preceding discussion of New Testament prophecy.

First, there is no reason to accept, but rather every reason to reject, the idea that New Testament prophecy lacks the infallibility of all other biblical prophecy. The distinction sought by the Continuationists is not to be found in Scripture. It contradicts or ignores the clear implications of Scripture at many points.

Second, this means all professed prophecy must be held to the standard of Deuteronomy 18:15-22. Such prophecy must be prepared to pass the test of absolute infallibility. If a prophet cannot pass this test, he or she must repent of and renounce the claim to prophetic status. As the argument of the Continuationists themselves assumes, this would eliminate most claims to the gift of prophecy today.

Third, a study of the biblical data regarding prophecy shows how misguided is the assumption that New Testament prophecy is equivalent to what is more properly called Spirit-anointed preaching. New Testament prophecy must not be distinguished in its essential character from Old Testament prophecy. This means the tests for true prophecy found in Deuteronomy 18:15-22 are normative for all biblical prophecy. There is not a single passage in the New Testament where the biblical terminology related to prophecy or prophesying refers to anything but the inspired reception and utterance of direct revelation.[15] There is not one reference that differs from the Old Testament identification of the prophet as the spokesman and mouth of God. We can certainly appreciate the high view of preaching which led the Puritans to speak of it as prophesying. Such a high view of preaching is certainly needed in our day. This accommodation and misuse of the biblical word was no doubt a little thing in the day of the Puritans. We remember, however, a statement made by one of the church fathers with regard to the earlier, defective statements of the doctrine of the Trinity: *What was a little thing then is a little thing no longer!*

With these Continuationist objections cleared away we are now able to see the powerful arguments for the cessation of the gift of prophecy in a clear light. We come to those arguments in the next chapter.

1 Sinclair B. Ferguson, *The Holy Spirit* (Downers Grove, IL: InterVarsity Press, 1996), pp. 226-228, finds this interpretation plausible. It is defended with ability by Robert L. Reymond, What about Continuing Revelations and Miracles in the Presbyterian Church Today? (Phillipsburg, NJ: Presbyterian and Reformed, 1977), pp. 32-34 and by Douglas Judisch, An Evaluation of Claims to the Charismatic Gifts (Grand Rapids: Baker Book House, 1978), pp. 45-54.

2 In this regard I believe Grudem's arguments in his *Systematic Theology,* pp.1032-1034, are quite cogent. I will not take the time to refute in detail the arguments of Cessationists who take this to refer to the completion of the canon. I see no need to do this because, if they are correct, they simply bolster my position. I mean no disrespect to the careful arguments of Reymond, Judisch, and others. I simply find their arguments unconvincing.

3 The Greek word is the plural, προφητεῖαι

4 The phrase, "we prophesy in part," clearly does not refer to prophecy as a partial gift, but to the partial knowledge communicated through the gift.

5 D. A. Carson, *Showing the Spirit: A Theological Exposition of 1 Corinthians 12-14* (Grand Rapids: Baker Book House, 1987), p. 70, though not a Cessationist, still remarks that these words do not "necessarily mean that a charismatic gift could not have been withdrawn earlier than the parousia."

6 I am happy to say that the view of 1 Corinthians 13:8-13 that I defend here seems to be the view of the well-known defender of Cessationism, Dr. Richard B. Gaffin, *Perspectives on Pentecost* (N. P.: Presbyterian and Reformed, 1979), p. 111.

7 Grudem, *Systematic Theology,* pp.1039-1040.

8 Wayne A. Grudem, *The Gift of Prophecy in the New Testament and Today* (Westchester, IL: Crossway Books, 1988), pp.93-104. Note Gaffin's response to this view of Agabus in *Are Miraculous Gifts for Today: Four Views,* pp.49-51.

9 We must, of course distinguish Agabus' prophecy from the attempts of Paul's friends to dissuade him from going to Jerusalem. The infallibility of the prophecy does not imply that their interpretation of its practical application was correct.

10 *The Infallible Word,* 3rd rev. ed. (Phillipsburg, NJ: Presbyterian and Reformed, 1978) p.11. Here John Murray argues this very point with regard to the instances of error the adversaries of inerrancy find in the Scriptures.

11 Grudem, *Systematic Theology,* p.1052, cites Acts 21:4 as proof of his view. This text says the disciples "kept telling Paul through the Spirit (δια τοῦ πνεύματος) not to set foot in Jerusalem." Grudem thinks this means they prophesied that Paul should not go to Jerusalem (and, since he continued his journey, Paul

disregarded as fallible this part of their prophecy). Actually, the use of δια τοῦ πνεύματος need not imply this at all. It may only mean they told Paul "on account of the Spirit" or "in connection with the Spirit" that he should not go to Jerusalem. Both these translations reflect legitimate ways of understanding *dia.* (Cf. 1 Timothy 2:15..) Dia. need not mean "through" here. Thus, what they told Paul was "on account of" or "in connection with" prophecy, but was not itself prophecy. Additionally, it is unlikely Luke means to imply that the disciples who told Paul this were prophets as Grudem's interpretation of the text implies. Note Acts 21:11-14, which continues this theme.

12   Ferguson, *The Holy Spirit,* p.219.

13   *The Infallible Word*, p.11.

14   In teaching this material I have been asked several times about the popular distinction between prophecy as foretelling and prophecy as forthtelling. In the present connection this popular distinction seems to imply that, while prophecy as foretelling must be inspired and infallible, prophecy as forthtelling may not be. Thus prophecy as forthtelling would be equivalent to preaching. The biblical data looked at in this and the preceding chapters shows that all prophecy (whether foretelling or forthtelling) is by virtue of being true prophecy inspired and infallible. It is communicated directly from God to the prophet and the prophet speaks it as the mouth of God. Prophecy may include both foretelling and forthtelling. The foretelling aspect of it is simply the sign and evidence that the entire prophecy (both foretelling and forthtelling) is inspired and infallible. I think that distinguishing prophecy into foretelling and forthtelling, though in a sense valid, is often both unhelpful and misleading. True prophecy is always inspired and infallible. True preaching is not.

CHAPTER 6

NEW TESTAMENT PROPHETS

Arguments for their Cessation

Rebutting the arguments for the continuation of New Testament prophecy required us to refer again and again to the foundation laid in our chapter on Old Testament prophecy. This illustrates how crucial the solid foundation of an understanding of Old Testament prophecy is in our approach to this matter. That foundation lies beneath the arguments brought forward in this chapter for the cessation of New Testament prophecy.

The New Testament prophets were foundational.

We noted earlier that Ephesians 2:20 clearly asserts the apostles were the foundation of Christ's church. We also noted that this must be given an historical interpretation that confines the apostolate to the early—first century—period of the church's existence. Now we must observe that the New Testament prophets are also said, in the same passage, to be the foundation of Christ's church. The passage does, as a matter of fact, read that the church is built "on the foundation of the apostles *and prophets*" (Emphasis mine). Since this is so, we have the same reason to conclude the cessation of prophets from this passage as we did to conclude the cessation of apostles.

Grudem, however, argues that the words, "and prophets,"[1] are explanatory. Thus, they should be read, "the apostles even prophets." Daniel B. Wallace, in his *Greek Grammar Beyond the Basics*, argues that such a grammatical construction of the Greek is wrong.[2] Additionally, the order (apostles then prophets) corresponds to that of Ephesians 3:5; 4:11; and 1 Corinthians 12:28-29.

> Ephesians 3:5—which in other generations was not made known to the sons of men, as it has now been revealed to His holy apostles and prophets in the Spirit.

> Ephesians 4:11—And He gave some as apostles, and some as prophets, and some as evangelists, and some as pastors and teachers.

> I Corinthians 12:28-29—And God has appointed in the church, first apostles, second prophets, third teachers, then miracles, then gifts of healings, helps, administrations, various kinds of tongues. All are not apostles, are they? All are not prophets, are they? All are not teachers, are they? All are not workers of miracles, are they?

In each of these parallel passages two things become absolutely clear. First, the prophets are distinct from the apostles—observe how the listing of the gifts in Ephesians 4:11 and 1 Corinthians 12:28-29 assumes this. Second, they are New Testament (not Old Testament) prophets. Observe here the statement of Ephesians 3:5 indicating that the mystery "in other generations was not made known to the sons of men, as it has *now* been revealed to His holy apostles and prophets in the Spirit." The entire force of the passage, and especially the now, shows that the prophets in question cannot be Old Testament prophets. This passage is quite significant because it occurs in such close proximity to Ephesians 2:20. Furthermore, the parallel order of apostles then prophets by itself suggests that it is New Testament prophets who are in view. We would have expected the order, prophets and apostles, if Old Testament prophets were the reference.[3] It is clear as well that the mention in Ephesians 4:11 of prophets in the listing of apostles, prophets, evangelists, and pastor-teachers refers to New Testament prophets.

Grudem's esoteric and peculiar interpretation of Ephesians 2:20 faces enormous difficulties on many fronts. That a fine theologian like Grudem opts for it illustrates the exegetical lengths to which one must go to defend Continuationism.

The prophets of Ephesians 2:20 are clearly *New Testament prophets*. They are neither *Old Testament prophets*, nor *New Testament apostles*. Thus, our argument that New Testament prophets are foundational for the church remains valid. It can be helpfully illustrated in the following diagram:

THE FOUNDATION OF THE PROPHETS (EPH. 2:20)

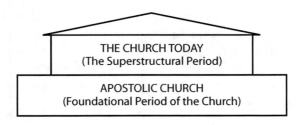

THE CHURCH TODAY
(The Superstructural Period)

APOSTOLIC CHURCH
(Foundational Period of the Church)

The New Testament prophets were infallible.

We have seen that the prophetic office conferred divine and infallible authority on the true prophet (Deut. 18:15ff.). This means that claims to prophecy today must be prepared to meet the standards of Deuteronomy 13 and 18 or be given up. Remember the inevitable conclusion we were forced to draw from those passages in chapter four:

> Putting these two passages together, we can say a true prophet possesses, and must possess, both of two infallible marks. First, what he prophesies must always come true. Second, he must not contradict previous revelation, but teach people to follow the true God (the God revealed through Moses).

The only alternative to meeting these standards is the condemnation of the Word of God. Most Continuationists do not believe that contemporary prophecy meets such standards. The widespread attempts among Continuationists to find warrant for an inferior form of prophecy in the Scriptures testify to this.

The New Testament prophets were canonical.

We have seen that the form of the Old Testament canon was Moses and the prophets. Indeed, in some cases, we have seen the entire Old Testament referred to as the "prophetic word" (2 Pet. 1:19-21). While not all prophecy in the Old Testament found its way into the canon, all such prophecy was in principle canonical and carried canonical authority with the people of God. Similarly, not all apostolic writings were preserved by the Holy Spirit to be put into the New Testament as we know it. Yet, as we have seen, all apostolic writings as the words of Christ's inspired representatives were in principle, canonical. If they had been preserved, of necessity they would have been part of our New Testaments.

What is the point? It is simply that if biblical prophecy exists today and can be verified as such, it is canonical. If it is canonical, then the canon is not closed, but open. The fact is, however, every Christian knows, and the contents of the New Testament plainly testify, that the canon of the New Testament is closed and has been closed for almost two thousand years.

The choice for Continuationists is stark. They may maintain their claims to continuing prophecy in the church, or they may have a closed canon. They may have continuing prophecy, or they may have the witness of the New Testament that the principle of canonical authority departed from the church nearly two thousand years ago.

Neil Babcock gives practical and experiential clout to the above arguments in his book *My Search for Charismatic Reality*. His words illustrate the agony a true Christian heart feels and ought to feel at false claims to prophetic revelation.

> Thus saith the Lord. How I struggled with those words! As Jacob wrestled with the angel in the dark of the night, so I wrestled with those words. As the angel wounded Jacob, so those words wounded me. And as Jacob's defeat became his victory, I thank God those words, so right and unfathomable in their significance, defeated me. The moment of truth came when I heard a prophecy spoken at a charismatic church I was visiting. I was sitting in the church trying to worship God while dreading the approach of that obligatory moment of silence which signaled that a prophecy was about to be spoken. The silence came, and soon it was broken by a bold and commanding "thus saith the Lord!"
> Those words triggered an immediate reaction. Conviction, like water rising against a dam, began to fill my soul. "Listen my people . . ." Until finally, the dam burst: "This is not my God," I cried within my heart. "This is not my Lord!"[4]

1   Grudem, *The Gift of Prophecy in the New Testament*, pp.45-63.

2   Daniel B. Wallace, *Greek Grammar Beyond the Basics* (Grand Rapids: Zonder-van, 1996), pp. 284-286.

3   This is, in fact, the order we find in 2 Peter 3:2, where Old Testament prophets are in view: "that you should remember the words spoken beforehand by the holy prophets and the commandment of the Lord and Savior spoken by your apostles."

4   Neil Babcock, *My Search for Charismatic Reality* (London: The Wakeman Trust, 1992), pp.58-59. One of my initial readers made this comment on Babcock's words: "I can identify with Mr. Babcock. I too have claimed "Thus saith the Lord" in a group or church setting. Although sincere and enthusiastic, I am ashamed and deeply saddened by such a claim. I now recoil at the thought."

PART 3

TONGUES SPEAKERS

CHAPTER 7

TONGUES AND TONGUES SPEAKERS

In this chapter we come to the next waterfall in the Cascade Argument against Continuationism. We have seen that Apostles of Christ do not continue in the church today. Building on that pivotal premise, we have argued that prophets also do not continue. With these presuppositions firmly established, we now come to consider the gift of tongues-speakers.

In certain respects, tongues-speaking is especially identified with the Charismatic movement. There are a number of important Charismatic claims concerning tongues-speaking that will not be directly addressed in this chapter. In many Continuationist churches, for instance, it is viewed as the sign of the baptism of the Spirit. It is not the purpose of this chapter to discuss the question of whether tongues-speaking is the indicator of the baptism of the Spirit. Nevertheless, I am bringing forward considerations that will profoundly influence one's view of this matter. For, if there are no tongues-speakers today, it certainly cannot be the present sign of the baptism of the Spirit—however that baptism is understood.

The major question taken up here is the one which advances the argument of this book: Do tongues-speakers continue in the church today? This question cannot, however, be separated from several others that have an impact on how it is answered. In this chapter we will discuss these questions: 1. *Were tongues human languages?* 2. *What were the rules about tongues-speaking in church?* 3. *Are there tongues-speakers today?* 4. *How should we explain contemporary tongues-speaking?*

Were tongues human languages?

The short answer is: Yes!. How have I arrived at such a confident answer? That takes a little longer to explain. It is important to notice at the outset of this explanation that tongues-speaking is only mentioned in the New Testament in Acts chapters 2, 10, 19 and 1 Corinthians chapters 12 through 14. This being premised, let us consider several things.[1]

In Acts 2, the first and pivotal reference in the Bible, tongues were clearly human languages.

No Continuationist should dispute the idea that the events of the Day of Pentecost recorded in Acts 2 are pivotal for understanding the gift of the Spirit.[2] In Acts 2 we have the first reference to the gift of tongues in the Bible. The phenomenon recorded in Acts 2 is the fulfillment of an ancient prophecy of the giving of the Spirit to the church. This prophecy is found in Joel 2:28-29 and came to manifest fruition in the gift of tongues. The outpouring of the Spirit recorded here is a once-for-all, epochal, or redemptive-historical event of the same kind as the incarnation, crucifixion, and resurrection of the Christ.[3] Like these events, it lays the foundation or sets the stage for the entire Christian era. Yet Acts 2:1-13 makes it very clear that the tongues spoken were human languages. Notice especially verses five through eleven:

> Now there were Jews living in Jerusalem, devout men from every nation under heaven. 6 And when this sound occurred, the crowd came together, and were bewildered because each one of them was hearing them speak in his own language. 7 They were amazed and astonished, saying, "Why, are not all these who are speaking Galileans? 8 "And how is it that we each hear them in our own language to which we were born? 9 "Parthians and Medes and Elamites, and residents of Mesopotamia, Judea and Cappadocia, Pontus and Asia, 10 Phrygia and Pamphylia, Egypt and the districts of Libya around Cyrene, and visitors from Rome, both Jews and proselytes, 11 Cretans and Arabs—we hear them in our own tongues speaking of the mighty deeds of God."

Given the indisputable precedent of Acts 2, there is every reason to conclude that the other instances of tongues-speaking in Acts (Acts 10:46; 19:6) were also human languages. Acts 2 sets a precedent for the meaning of tongues in Acts (and the rest of the New Testament). This precedent, I submit, must control how we interpret the other mentions of the gift of tongues in Acts. It would take the strongest evidence to overturn this presumption. As a matter of fact, no evidence of any kind exists to show that the tongues of Acts 10:46 and 19:6 were anything else than foreign languages.

It is sometimes argued that the miracle of Acts 2 was not tongues-speaking, but tongues-hearing, but this is clearly wrong.
This interpretation is put forward in order to distinguish the miracle of Acts 2 from that mentioned in 1 Corinthians 12-14. The supposed proof for this interpretation is the emphasis in Acts 2:8 and 11 on how all the different nationalities *heard* the apostles speaking in their own languages. The problem with this interpretation is twofold. First, the gift is called tongues—*not ears* (Acts 2:4, 6)! Second, the passage explicitly says that they *spoke* in other tongues (Acts 2:4, 6).

The word "tongues" was often used in the New Testament to refer to human languages (Rev. 5:9; 7:9).
A tongue in the language of the New Testament was not just an organ in our mouths. It was a human language. Wherever a physical tongue is not in view, this seems to be the default meaning of the word. Here are two examples of this use of the word.[4]

> Revelation 5:9—And they sang a new song, saying, "Worthy are You to take the book and to break its seals; for You were slain, and purchased for God with Your blood men from every tribe and tongue and people and nation."

> Revelation 7:9—After these things I looked, and behold, a great multitude which no one could count, from every nation and all tribes and peoples and tongues, standing before the throne and before the Lamb, clothed in white robes, and palm branches were in their hands...

Though 1 Corinthians 13:1 refers to the "tongues of ... angels," it need not be understood to mean that the gift of tongues in Corinth was an angelic, heavenly, ecstatic, prayer language.
Paul says, "*If* I speak with the tongues of ... angels ..." (1 Cor. 13:1—Emphasis mine). From this text Continuationists argue that tongues are heavenly languages. Paul's statement, however, may be hyperbole

(as if he had said, *even if* I should speak with the tongues of angels). Alternatively, Paul's language may echo a claim by some Corinthian (perhaps a claim by one of the so-called apostles who opposed Paul) and not be designed to reveal the Apostle's doctrine. Thus, Paul would be saying, Suppose that I myself spoke with the tongues of angels—as you claim to do. Finally, we should remember that angels do not have bodies, tongues, or, therefore, spoken languages (Heb. 1:14).[5]

When 1 Corinthians 14:2 is thought to refer to a heavenly language, it is misinterpreted.
1 Corinthians 14:2 says, "one who speaks in a tongue does not speak to men but to God for no one understands." This only means, however, that no one understands—*if there is no interpretation!* God understands not because it is a heavenly language, but because God knows all human languages. Verse thirteen—remember—instructs the Corinthians, "Therefore let one who speaks in a tongue pray that he may interpret."

Paul's call for interpretation in 1 Corinthians 14:13, 26-28 seems to assume that the tongues here were human languages.
That the tongues were human languages is assumed by the call for interpretation. I do not deny, of course, that God could give the ability to interpret even a heavenly or angelic language. The statement more naturally refers, however, to the interpretation of a human language unknown to those present.

Paul's citation of Isaiah 28:11 in 1 Corinthians 14:21 indicates that the tongues mentioned here are human languages.
Paul cites Isaiah 28:11 in 1 Corinthians 14:21: "In the Law it is written, 'By men of strange tongues and by the lips of strangers I will speak to this people, and even so they will not listen to me,' says the LORD." The tongues of Isaiah 28:11 are foreign languages. It is difficult to see how this citation is pertinent to Paul's argument or relevant to his subject unless the tongues spoken in Corinth were human languages.

Paul's whole point in 1 Corinthians 14:21 is that the gift of tongues was a sign of judgment on the Jews.
Isaiah 28:11 refers to the tongue or language of a foreign army. The Jews hear it because that army has occupied the land of Israel as a foreign invasion force. This situation was a result of the judgment of God on

the Jews. It is difficult to see how hearing the gift of someone speaking in the tongues of angels could be considered a judgment. This would appear to be more of a blessing (like Paul's being caught up to the third heaven and hearing inexpressible things—2 Cor. 12:1-5) than a curse.

The meaning of the gift of tongues in the Bible includes the idea that it is "a reversal of Babel."

Tongues mark the reversal of Babel and the universality of the New Covenant. The curse of Babel divided the nations by imposing different languages (Gen. 11:1-9). When on the Day of Pentecost the Word of God was proclaimed in many tongues, this was a sign that the curse of Babel was now to be reversed. Many nations and peoples were to be reconciled in the one Christ and His work of redemption (Eph. 2:12-19). Thus, what was a judgment on the Jews was at the same time a blessing on the Gentiles. Sinclair Ferguson asserts:

> For Paul, tongues serve partly as the sign of God's judgment on his covenant people. What marks the reversal of Babel and indicates the universality of the new covenant also signals judgment on the covenant people for the rejection of the Christ. Babylon reversed is, in another sense, Jerusalem judged {'their loss means riches for the Gentiles'}, (Rom. 11:2).[6]

The significance of the tongues-speaking of the New Covenant in the biblical story is destroyed except on the supposition that tongues were foreign languages. Only the gift of speaking foreign languages reverses Babel and brings reconciliation to the nations.

Tongues are a spiritual gift given for the edification of the body.

The purpose of the spiritual gifts does not terminate on the welfare of the one to whom they are given. One major principle with regard to the gifts of the Spirit in general is reiterated several times in the New Testament. Gifts are given to individuals for the sake of the body of Christ (Eph. 4:11-13; 1 Cor. 12:7; 1 Pet. 4:10). Continuationists, however, sometimes present tongues as a private prayer language given to the individual for his own private edification.[7] Since the gifts of the Spirit are given for the edification of the body, it is strange to hear Continuationists arguing that tongues are a private prayer language. In whatever way 1 Corinthians 14:2, 4, 17, and 28 are to be properly understood, they cannot be intended to teach that tongues-speaking is mainly or exclusively a private prayer language.[8] Tongues-speaking must rather be primarily for the edification of the church as a whole. This is, in fact, the point Paul is making. To be of edification in the assembly of the church, he is saying, they must be interpreted.

CONCLUSION

If tongues were foreign languages that could be interpreted, then many, if not most, claims to the gift of tongues today are invalidated. They are not, and do not even claim to be, foreign languages.

What were the rules about tongues-speaking in church?

The theme of 1 Corinthians 14 is the regulation of spiritual gifts in the assemblies of the church. One of the major emphases of 1 Corinthians 14 is, therefore, to give rules for the use of the gifts of tongues in the meetings of the church. The rules for speaking in tongues are these:

Only two or three tongues-speakers could speak (and not at the same time) in any given meeting of the church so that order might be preserved (1 Cor. 14:27).

If tongues were to be spoken in the church, they had to be interpreted. If no one interpreted, the tongues-speaker had to keep silent (1 Cor. 14:28).

No woman was allowed to speak in tongues in the meeting of the church. This is the major reason for the prohibition of 1 Corinthians 14:34-35.[9]

CONCLUSION

It is obvious that few or none of these rules are observed in most of the churches where tongues-speaking is practiced. This is certainly a call for the reformation of such meetings. The regular and almost systematic violation of these biblical rules raises, however, a profound suspicion that the tongues phenomenon today is not scripturally based. When the clear rules of Scripture are so flagrantly disobeyed, it is right to wonder if Scripture has much to do with this practice at all.

Are tongues for today?

The gift of tongues-speakers does not exist in the church today. The argument for this conclusion is as follows: *Tongues-speaking was a form of prophecy and, therefore, when accompanied by the gift of interpretation, functionally equivalent to prophecy. As we have seen, there are no living prophets in the church today. Thus, neither can there be any tongues-speakers.*

The key to this argument is that tongues-speaking was a form of prophecy. How do we know this? There are several arguments.

The pivotal example of tongues-speaking in Acts 2 is identified as prophecy. Peter's explanation of the phenomenon in Acts 2:14-18 explains it by means of a prediction that refers to the outpouring of the Spirit in the gift of prophecy.

> But Peter, taking his stand with the eleven, raised his voice and declared to them: "Men of Judea and all you who live in Jerusalem, let this be known to you and give heed to my words. 15 "For these men are not drunk, as you suppose, for it is only the third hour of the day; 16 but this is what was spoken of through the prophet Joel: 17 'AND IT SHALL BE IN THE LAST DAYS,' God says, 'THAT I WILL POUR FORTH OF MY SPIRIT ON ALL MANKIND; AND YOUR SONS AND YOUR DAUGHTERS SHALL PROPHESY, AND YOUR YOUNG MEN SHALL SEE VISIONS, AND YOUR OLD MEN SHALL DREAM DREAMS; 18 EVEN ON MY BONDSLAVES, BOTH MEN AND WOMEN, I WILL IN THOSE DAYS POUR FORTH OF MY SPIRIT And they shall prophesy.'"

1 Corinthians 14:5 asserts the functional equivalence of tongues-speaking with prophecy—provided that someone interprets what is said. Paul declares, "Now I wish that you all spoke in tongues, but even more that you would prophesy; and greater is one who prophesies than one who speaks in tongues, unless he interprets, so that the church may receive edifying." The plain implication is that, if there is interpretation, tongues-speaking is just as great as prophesying. We have seen in previous chapters the exalted view of prophecy given us in Scripture. When Paul makes tongues-speaking equivalent to prophecy if it is interpreted, this exalts tongues-speaking to the level of infallible and direct revelation. Though tongues-speaking is clearly distinct from prophecy in that it involves the additional ability to speak in a language one has not learned, it is also substantially equivalent to prophecy in communicating the direct revelation that is given through prophecy.

In both prophecy and tongues the speaker is uttering mysteries (1 Cor. 13:2 with 14:2). Compare these two passages. 1 Corinthians

13:2 says, "If I have the gift of prophecy, and know all mysteries and all knowledge; and if I have all faith, so as to remove mountains, but do not have love, I am nothing." 1 Corinthians 14:2 remarks: "For one who speaks in a tongue does not speak to men but to God; for no one understands, but in his spirit he speaks mysteries." Both in prophecy and tongues a mystery is spoken. We know, however, that a mystery is the special content of prophecy. When Paul gives his prediction in 1 Corinthians 15:51, he says that he is telling them a mystery. "Behold, I tell you a mystery; we will not all sleep, but we will all be changed." Prophecy and mystery are also closely related in Romans 11:25; 16:25-26; Eph. 3:3; and in the Book of Revelation. The Book of Revelation was, of course, a prophecy (Rev. 1:3). Thus, throughout it contains mysteries (Rev. 1:20; 10:7; 17:5; 17:7).

Tongues and prophecy are closely associated with considerable frequency in the New Testament. Besides Acts 2, notice Acts 19:6; 1 Corinthians 13:1-2, 8; and in 1 Corinthians 14. This intimate association is easily explained if tongues-speaking was a form of prophecy.

For all these reasons, tongues is to be identified as a form of prophecy. Therefore, if prophecy has ceased, then so also has tongues. It may be for this reason that in the later books of the Apostle Paul (the Pastoral Epistles) there is no regulation or even mention of tongues-speaking. It was, like prophecy, passing away. At any rate, the substantial equivalency of tongues-speaking and prophesying cannot be missed in an unprejudiced examination of the New Testament.

How should we explain contemporary tongues-speaking?

Many apparently sincere Christians engage in (what they think is) tongues-speaking today. If the gift really has ceased in the church, how do we explain their experience? This is a serious question. If we reject the continuation of tongues-speakers in the church, must we conclude—as some do—that all such professing Christians are under the power of the devil or even demon-possessed? This would be a very serious charge to make. It would also be a charge that would tend to make charitable Christians reluctant to conclude that tongues-speakers no longer continue in the church. Is the stark alternative that professed tongues-speaking today is either divine or demonic? Thankfully, I do not think this is the choice that follows from the Cessationist position. It is important to remember the following things when the origin of the tongues practiced today is considered.

We do not as Christians build doctrine on experience, but on the

Bible. Thus, the experience and convictions of ever so many supposed tongues-speakers cannot be and is not normative for doctrine. Let God be true, and every man a liar!

Yet, this question may be asked: If professed tongues-speaking today is not a divine gift, where does it come from? Some of it may indeed be demonic. Demons are certainly capable of coming to church and enabling people to do things that they could not otherwise do (Mark 5:4-5; 2 Thess. 2:9).

Most may be a kind of natural phenomenon that does not need to be explained as either essentially or originally divine or demonic. This phenomenon may be called free vocalization and has been observed in completely non-Christian contexts.[10] As a natural phenomenon, it need not be condemned as necessarily demonic.

I have already stated my intention to distinguish between miracle-workers and miracles, when we come to that part of the argument. This discussion is reserved for the next chapter. Could, however, such a distinction be applied here? Is there, in other words, the possibility that a Cessationist might allow that on rare occasions God might give someone the ability to speak a foreign language they have not learned in the normal way? Such a "miracle" would have to be distinguished clearly from biblical tongues-speaking. Is it possible, however, that God might do something like this for a missionary on one occasion without that person having the gift of tongues-speaking in the biblical sense? With careful qualification it may be possible to answer yes to such questions. Such a "miracle" would not involve prophetic status for what was spoken or a number of the other distinctives of the biblical gift of tongues-speaking. The advantage of affirming such a carefully qualified "miracle" as this would be the possibility of explaining certain instances of supposed "tongues-speaking" as "miraculous" without affirming that tongues-speakers are given to the church today.

1   There is a disputed reference to "new tongues" in Mark 16:17. The problem is whether the ending of Mark in which this reference is found is authentic. Many of the earliest texts of the New Testament do not contain the passage in which this reference is found.

2   In light of the evidence I am about to give for the pivotal importance of the Day of Pentecost, I am amazed that C. Samuel Storms in *Are Miraculous Gifts for Today?* (Grand Rapids: Zondervan, 1996), p. 220, can say that "there is no reason to think Acts 2, rather than, say 1 Corinthians 14, is the standard by which all occurrences of this phenomenon must be judged."

3   I do not mean to prejudge or decide all the issues that separate Cessationist and Continuationist about the giving of the Spirit on the Day of Pentecost by describing that event as once-for-all, epochal, and redemptive-historical. I am only emphasizing its pivotal importance in the biblical story.

4   Not counting Mark 16:17, there are 49 uses of the word, tongue, in the New Testament. Seventeen appear to refer to a physical tongue. Seven clearly refer to a language. The remaining 25 refer to the gift of speaking in tongues. Five of these are in Acts and clearly refer to a human language. The remaining 20 are the uses that are disputed. All these uses are in 1 Corinthians. Also in 1 Corinthians 14:21 the compound word, ἑτερογλώσσοις—strange-tongues, occurs. It is used in the translation of an Old Testament text that clearly refers to a foreign human language.

5   One of my initial readers asked this question: "Is this always true? Can they not take the form and faculties of a man?" It is true that angels can take the form and faculties of a man. I would maintain, however, that when they do this they also take his tongue or language. If an angel takes a human form, he also takes a human language so that he can speak to those to whom he is sent.

6   Sinclair Ferguson, The Holy Spirit, (Downers Grove, IL: InterVarsity Press, 1996), p.213.

7   This seems to be the main importance which Storms (Are Miraculous Gifts for Today?, p.222) attaches to the gift of tongues. "I want to conclude this discussion of tongues on a personal note by simply saying that I have found this gift to be profoundly helpful in my prayer life. It has served only to deepen my intimacy with the Lord Jesus Christ and to enhance my zeal and joy in worship. Caricatures notwithstanding, praying in the Spirit does not diminish one's capacity for rational thought or commitment to the authority of the written Word of God."

8   1 Corinthians 14:2, 4, 17, and 28 are often cited as proof that the tongues-speaking of 1 Corinthians 12-14 was a private prayer language. The frequently intended implications of this are that (1) it is not given mainly for the edification of the church and (2) it may not be a human language at all. Paul only concedes, however, in these verses that tongues-speaking may edify oneself.

His main point is that without interpretation it does not edify the church. I do not deny that the exercise of spiritual gifts has the "fringe benefit" of edifying ourselves. (This is Richard Gaffin's phraseology in Are Miraculous Gifts for Today?, pp. 294-295.) The preacher frequently edifies himself when he preaches. The one who uses his gift for evangelism to speak to unbelievers about Christ often edifies himself. The point is that this is not the main benefit of these gifts, but a fringe benefit. The gifts were given primarily for the good of others—not for one's own good. This being the case, Paul's concession that one with the gift of tongues may edify himself contradicts neither the idea that the gift was given primarily for the edification of others, nor the idea that it is a human language.

9   Wayne Grudem, *The Gift of Prophecy in 1 Corinthians* (Washington, D. C.: University Press of America, 1982), pp. 242-255, argues that 1 Cor. 14:33b-35 simply forbids women to engage in judging the prophets (1 Cor. 14:29b). Though his argument is ingenious, it is completely unconvincing. It is impossible in the present limited context to demonstrate thoroughly all the reasons why this is so. The major reason, however, is that his interpretation ignores the contextual use of both λαλεω (speak) and σιγαω (keep silent). The verb λαλεω (speak) used in 1 Cor. 14:34-35 is used 24 times in 1 Corinthians 14. Eighteen times it refers to tongues-speaking, two times to prophesying (vv. 3 and 29), and 2 times (vv. 6 and 19) to general speaking or teaching. The verb σιγαω (keep silent) is used in tandem with λαλεω in verses 28, 30, and 34. (These are its only uses in 1 Corinthians 14.) It is used to command tongues-speakers, prophets, and women in turn not to speak in the assemblies of the church, but to keep silent. The use of both these verbs in this context, then, tend to support the view that in 1 Cor. 14:34-35, Paul is forbidding women to prophesy and to speak in tongues in the church. In contrast, these verbs are never used with reference to judging the prophets. These facts by themselves are fatal for Grudem's view. Grudem, however, rejects this interpretation on the grounds that it conflicts with 1 Cor. 11:5 and 1 Cor. 14:23-31. If 1 Corinthians 11:5 referred to women praying or prophesying in meetings of the church, Grudem might be right to see a conflict. The fact is, however, that there is no evidence that 1 Cor. 11:2-16 refers to meetings of the church. It likely has reference to less formal, public situations. The more formal, church situation is in view in 1 Cor. 14:33b-35—as Paul makes clear by his threefold use of the word church. As for 1 Cor. 14:23-31, the seemingly blanket permission for all to minister in the meetings of the church is clearly being qualified in verses 27-35. Furthermore, the "alls" and "eaches" of the previous verses are clearly hyperbolical. Paul clearly did not believe that all could speak in tongues (v. 23) or that all could prophesy (v. 24). He acknowledges that all did not even possess these gifts (1 Cor. 12:31 and 14:1). Finally, when Paul says in v. 31, "you can all prophesy," he is referring to prophets (v. 29) and not prophetesses (Luke 2:36; Rev. 2:20; Acts 21:19).

10   Sinclair Ferguson, *The Holy Spirit*, p.234; C. S. Butler, *Test the Spirits* (Welwyn, Herts: Evangelical Press, 1985), pp. 44-47

PART 4

MIRACLE-WORKERS

CHAPTER 8

MIRACLE-WORKERS AND MIRACLES

INTRODUCTION

The Distinction between Miracles and Miracle-workers

This final part of our study of miraculous gifts takes up the subject of miracle-workers. It is the last of the series of waterfalls in our Cascade Argument against the extraordinary gifts being in the church today. The following diagram (which the reader has seen before) summarizes the argument so far and brings us to the present chapter on miracle-workers and miracles.[1]

THE CASCADE ARGUMENT

We begin with the mention of miracle-workers in 1 Corinthians 12:28-29.

> And God has appointed in the church, first apostles, second prophets, third teachers, then miracles, then gifts of healings, helps,

> administrations, various kinds of tongues. 29 All are not apostles, are
> they? All are not prophets, are they? All are not teachers, are they?
> All are not workers of miracles, are they?

In 1 Corinthians 12:28 it seems that this gift is called simply miracles, but notice something very important. The gift of which we are speaking is not simply miracles.[2] According to verse twenty-nine (as translated by the NASB) the gift is *miracle-workers*. Though the word in the original is simply miracles, in the NASB it is translated *workers of miracles*. This is not a translation that takes undue license with the original. It is rather a very necessary way of translating the original. The context forces us to this translation because of the wording of the original. It literally reads, as you see, *All are not miracles?* This is nonsense and cannot possibly be the right translation. In parallel with the other questions in verse twenty-nine and thirty, we must read: *All are not miracle-workers, are they?* [3]

My point is that the issue before us is not whether there are miracles in the church today. I, together with many other Cessationists, affirm that God may do miracles today. The question is rather whether there are miracle-workers today. It is whether there are those with the gift of working miracles. It is one thing for there to be miracles. It is another for there to be the gift of working miracles or *miracle-workers*. This is a distinction that is crucially important for the subject before us. What I intend to argue is that there are no miracle-workers—no Christians gifted to perform miracles. [4]

The distinction I am making may be helpfully clarified by a true story. C. Samuel Storms in his defense of Continuationism uses this historical example.[5] He cites the example of C. H. Spurgeon, the great Reformed Baptist preacher of the mid-nineteenth century. A number of times in preaching Spurgeon appeared to speak to his hearers with supernatural insight. He would strikingly and particularly describe the sins and circumstances of individuals unknown to him who were sitting in his congregations. This sometimes led to the conversion of those individuals. These may be instances in which Spurgeon was miraculously guided in his choice of illustrations and words. It does not trouble this Cessationist to admit that here we have a miracle (especially since—like Spurgeon—I am a Reformed Baptist). What, however, Storms does not show and cannot show is that Spurgeon ever claimed on the basis of these events to be a prophet or miracle-worker

(Because, of course, he did not). I wonder if there were many times when Spurgeon used the same exact kind of language in which no one matching his description was present. Perhaps there were many such times. Storms certainly cannot prove that there were not. The point is God may have performed miracles in connection with Spurgeon's ministry, but this fact did not make Spurgeon a miracle-worker.

The Definition of Miracles

Christians ordinarily assume that everyone knows what a miracle is. The fact is, however, that it is no easy matter to define a miracle. One problem is: Are miracles uniquely acts of God? Christians reject the idea that nature is something alien to God and in which He is uninvolved. We refuse the teaching of Deism that God is distant and removed from His creation. We rather see God's hand in the ordinary events of nature and history, as well as in miracles. Thus, the question must be asked, "What is the difference between God's powerful working in creation all the time and God's powerful working in a miracle?" Many such problems as this confront a biblical theology of miracles.

For our purposes a significant problem is that in neither Greek nor Hebrew is there an exact equivalent to our English word, miracle.[6] Rather in both languages there are at least four words which—especially when used in the plural—refer to what we call miracles. Those words are works, powers, wonders, and signs. The difficulty is that our English word, miracle, is commonly used to cover events that go beyond the technical use of these words in the Bible. Miracle, in other words, has in English a broader connotation and designation than the biblical words in terms of which a miracle is often defined. For instance, in the Bible neither God's original work of creation out of nothing, nor His work of regeneration in the heart of a sinner is described by means of the words just mentioned. When we speak of a miracle, however, we often refer to any event that displays God's omnipotence or supernatural power— ordinarily including both creation and regeneration. Theologians who define miracle strictly in terms of the biblical words just mentioned categorize such events as extraordinary providences rather than miracles. I think it is wise to recognize that miracle is an English word with a meaning not exactly equivalent to any biblical word. If it is used more broadly, it may refer to any unusual exhibition of the extraordinary providence or supernatural power of God. In this broad sense, I am happy to affirm that God does miracles today. It is possible, however, to define *miracle* more strictly. In this more strict sense there is reason to say that miracles do not occur today. Here is why.

Miracle is used in different translations of the English Bible to translate a specific collection of biblical words: *works, powers, wonders, and signs.* A strict definition based on this terminology is this. *A miracle is a redemptive, revelatory, extraordinary, external, astonishing manifestation of the power of God.*

Let me break this definition down and show how it embodies the biblical terminology.

A miracle is a *manifestation of the power of God.* (It is a display of divine work or power.)

A miracle is *astonishing.* (It is a wonder.)

A miracle takes place in the *external* realm. (The Bible seems to reserve these words for things that become visible in the physical world. The new birth may be popularly described as a miracle. It is certainly an operation of God's supernatural power. The Bible, however, reserves its technical terminology for miracles for something in itself visible or external. Since the new birth takes place in the hidden regions of the heart, it does not qualify as a biblical miracle in this precise or technical sense.)[7]

It is *extraordinary.* God works in an ordinary (well-known, commonly experienced) way all the time in creation. A miracle occurs when God does something extra-ordinary.

It is *revelatory.* It is a sign done by a prophet or apostle to attest the divine origin of his message.

A miracle is *redemptive.* The miracles of the Bible—God's works, powers, wonders, and signs—are connected with the work of redemption.

As I shall expand upon below, strictly speaking a biblical miracle is a miraculous sign done by a miracle-worker to attest the divine revelation of which he is the messenger. That is why in the strict sense of the word I am forced to affirm that there are no miracles today.

With all this providing a formative structure for our study of miracle-workers, I have three points to make in this chapter.

Miracle-workers did not arise with regular frequency in biblical times, but were concentrated at certain momentous periods in biblical history.[8]

There are long periods in history in which few or no miracle-workers are mentioned. From creation to the period of the flood (fifteen hundred years), from the period of the flood to the period of Abraham (four hundred years), the whole time of Israel's stay in Egypt (two hundred fifteen years), and during the Inter-Testamental period (four hundred years) few or no biblical miracles are recorded. Thus, for at least half of the period of history before the First Advent of Christ, we know of no miracle-workers.

Strictly speaking, biblical miracles are called signs, as well as wonders, powers, and works, and thus were intended to attest the new revelation given through the miracle-worker.[9]
A summary of the biblical use of the words for miracles shows miracles were given to attest the redemptive revelation being given through the miracle-worker. Miraculous signs attested Moses (Ex. 4:1-5; Deut. 34:10-12). Miraculous signs also attested the Old Testament prophets (Deut. 13:1-5; 18:15-22; 1 Kings 18:36; Psa. 74:9).

In the New Testament the same correlation is clear. Miraculous signs attested Jesus, the Messiah (John 2:11; 5:36). Miraculous signs also attested the Apostles of Christ. The miraculous signs they themselves did attested them (2 Cor. 12: 12; Heb. 2:3-4). The unique power to impart to others the ability to do miraculous signs attested them (Acts 8:1-24). Miraculous signs also attested the apostles' representatives and New Testament prophets (Acts 6:5, 8; 8:1-13; 1 Cor. 13:2; 14:24, 25).

Finally, deceptive miraculous signs attest false christs and false apostles and their lying message (Matt. 24:24; 2 Thess. 2:9-12; Rev. 13:13-14).

The conclusion that this data leads us to is this: In the Bible miracles (strictly defined) definitely occur in conjunction with those who are the organs of new or direct revelation. If we believe that God is no longer giving such revelation, then we should expect a complete cessation of miracles in this stricter sense of the word.

REVELATION AND MIRACLES

Revelation ←·····→ Miracles

No Revelation ←·····→ No Miracles

Miracle-workers performing miraculous signs have ceased.
Why must we say that miracle-workers performing miraculous signs have ceased? If we believe that miraculous signs attesting miracle-

workers continue, then we have thereby committed ourselves to continuing redemptive revelation. This would entail the implication that the canon is not closed. If we believe in miracle-workers, then we commit ourselves to the idea that there are divinely attested apostles or prophets in the world to whom we must give belief and obedience. Again, on this view the canon is not closed.

All the key biblical passages tie miraculous signs to redemptive revelation and identify miracle-workers as organs of direct revelation. Moses, the prophets in the Old Testament, Jesus, the apostles, and the New Testament prophets worked miracles in order to give divine attestation to the revelation they bring. Biblical miracles are signs intended to identify, attest, and to some degree, embody that revelation.

Are there miracles today?

I am not denying by all this that there are miracles in the world today in the broader sense of supernatural occurrences and extraordinary providences. I am only saying that there are no miracles in the stricter sense. There are no miracle-workers performing miraculous signs to attest the redemptive revelation they bring from God. Though God has never locked Himself out of His world and is still at liberty to do as He pleases, when He pleases, how He pleases, and where He pleases, He has made it clear that the progress of redemptive revelation attested by miraculous signs done by miracle-workers has been brought to conclusion in the revelation embodied in our New Testaments.

1   Someone may wonder about healers and healings. I include them in the broad-
    er category dealt with in this chapter: miracle-workers and miracles.

2   The Greek word is δυνάμεις which literally means powers. There is no single
    Greek word that exactly translates our English word, miracles. *Powers* is one
    of several Greek words that sometimes approximate the meaning of miracle in
    English. The others are signs (σημεῖα), wonders (τέρατα), and works (εργα).

3   It is possible that the same translation is appropriate in verse twenty eight..
    While the first three gifts in the list refer to the people who are the gifts, with
    miracles the list begins to name abilities as the gifts (miracles, gifts of heal-
    ing, administrations etc.). Perhaps in light of verse twenty nine here too the
    translation should be miracle-workers, those with gifts of healing, those with
    administrative abilities.

4   This is Gaffin's argument as well in *Are Miraculous Gifts for Today?*, pp.41-42.
    He distinguishes between miracles and those gifted to perform miracles.

5   *Are Miraculous Gifts for Today?*, pp.201-203.

6   Something of the problem with the use of the English word, *miracle*, to translate
    biblical words for miracles may be exhibited in the following facts. The NASB
    uses miracle, miracles, and miraculous thirty one times. It translates power or
    powers twenty-two times. It translates sign or signs two times. It translates
    wonder or wonders seven times. The KJV uses "miracle" and "miracles," but
    not "miraculous," a total of thirty-seven times. It translates no Greek word one
    time, "wonder" or "wonders" three times, "sign" or "signs" twenty-four times,
    power or powers nine times. NIV uses the words "miracle," " miracles," and
    "miraculous" one hundred four times; NKJV sixteen times; ASV nine times;
    RSV thirteen times. Clearly, the equivalence of "miracle" to any of the words in
    biblical languages is a matter of diverse opinion among translators.

7   It is important to realize that when the Bible uses work and power in the singu-
    lar, it may not be referring to miracles. It is when these words are used in the
    plural—works and powers—that they become technical terms for miracles.

8   Ferguson, *The Holy Spirit*, p.224.

9   Ibid, pp.224-225.

CONCLUSION

CHAPTER 9

HAS
THE
GLORY
DEPARTED?

INTRODUCTION

Cascading from the cessation of the apostolate, the arguments against the continuation of prophets, tongues-speakers, and miracle-workers have poured down in one waterfall after another. I hope that this argument has seemed as unstoppable to you as the tons of water that cascade over Niagara Falls.

But even if it has, I foresee that some may feel a sense of frustration. "No apostles! No prophets! No tongues-speakers! No miracle-workers! I know what you are against. But what are you *for*?" Others may be convinced by the argument, but feel a kind of disappointment. "If the church has no living apostles, prophets, tongues-speakers, or miracle-workers, what does it have? Where is its glory? Where is its power?"

This book is not written for professional theologians who can sit in their ivory towers divorced from all such practical concerns. It is not written for those interested in theoretical arguments with no experiential results. Such theologians may not feel that these questions merit a response. I am interested in touching the hearts and minds of serious and practical Christians. This final chapter is dedicated to responding to the frustration and disappointment of such readers. But make no mistake! There is a satisfying and glorious response. It is derived from the words of Jesus Himself in Luke 16:19-31.

"Now there was a rich man, and he habitually dressed in purple and fine linen, joyously living in splendor every day. 20 "And a poor man named Lazarus was laid at his gate, covered with sores, 21 and longing to be fed with the crumbs which were falling from the rich man's table; besides, even the dogs were coming and licking his sores. 22 "Now the poor man died and was carried away by the angels to Abraham's bosom; and the rich man also died and was buried. 23 "In Hades he lifted up his eyes, being in torment, and saw Abraham far away and Lazarus in his bosom. 24 "And he cried out and said, 'Father Abraham, have mercy on me, and send Lazarus so that he may dip the tip of his finger in water and cool off my tongue, for I am in agony in this flame.' 25 "But Abraham said, 'Child, remember that during your life you received your good things, and likewise Lazarus bad things; but now he is being comforted here, and you are in agony. 26 'And besides all this, between us and you there is a great chasm fixed, so that those who wish to come over from here to you will not be able, and that none may cross over from there to us.' 27 "And he said, 'Then I beg you, father, that you send him to my father's house -- 28 for I have five brothers -- in order that he may warn them, so that they will not also come to this place of torment.' 29 "But Abraham said, 'They have Moses and the Prophets; let them hear them.' 30 "But he said, 'No, father Abraham, but if someone goes to them from the dead, they will repent!' 31 "But he said to him, 'If they do not listen to Moses and the Prophets, they will not be persuaded even if someone rises from the dead.'"

As I have said, I am conscious that to some the argument presented in this book may seem to strip the church of its glory, life, excitement, and power. Some will ask, "If we do not have miraculous gifts today, what shall we do? How shall we convince the unconverted of the truth of the gospel?" From where will the gospel receive its power? These are natural questions. They find their classic, biblical answer in the passage before us and in many others like it. From it I want to show you Jesus' teaching about the power and sufficiency of the Scriptures to authenticate themselves in the hearts of men.

The question answered in this passage is: What is it that proves to men that the Bible is the Word of God? Do we need miracles and signs today to authenticate its message? Do we need experts and relics? Do we need those famous evidences that demand a verdict? How do we know the Bible is God's Word?

Let me illustrate the question. To travel internationally, a passport is required. To enter another country, I need a passport from the United States of America. Rarely have I been more conscious of the privilege of being a citizen of the United States than when I have shown my United States passport as I have entered various countries. Especially important is the right this passport gives me to return to the United States of America. It authenticates me as a citizen of the United States and gives me the right to return to our wonderful country. In Luke 16:19-31 Jesus displays the passport of the Bible into the consciences of men. He tells us what gives it the right to enter the hearts of men and, with binding authority, call them to repentance. In so doing He reveals the glory, life, power, and sufficiency of the Word of God for the church. Those who feel that the absence of the miraculous gifts steals from the church its glory, life, and power should listen closely.

Consider five expository remarks about this passage and then several practical applications from it to the issue at hand.

EXPOSITORY REMARKS

The Sobering Context of This Teaching (Luke 16:19-26)

The solemn and sobering context of Jesus' teaching about the Bible is his teaching on the subject of hell. In the immediate context of this teaching several most solemn realities about hell have been seen.

The fact of hell has been mentioned. Verse twenty-three refers to Hades, the Greek word for hell.

The torment of hell for its inhabitants is emphasized. Verse twenty-three refers to the rich man being *tormented* in its flame.

The immutability (or unchanging character) of hell is displayed. Hell is a prison from which escape is eternally impossible. Verses twenty-five and twenty-six speak of the great gulf fixed between heaven and hell that prevents any escape from that terrible prison.

The sufficiency of the Scriptures to show themselves to be God's Word means nothing less than their ability to show themselves to be God's Word *with respect to such awesome realities*. It is the ability of the Scriptures so to show themselves to be God's Word as to be a sufficient warning against the danger of the eternal fire of hell. The question is, "Are the Scriptures sufficient for even this momentous purpose?"

The Implied Denial of This Teaching (Luke 16:27-28)

In verses twenty-seven and twenty-eight the rich man subtly and by way of implication denies that the Scriptures by themselves are a sufficient warning to flee from the wrath to come. This subtle denial becomes evident in the request of the rich man to send someone to warn his five still-living brothers.

It is made by the one in hell. This alone should make us suspect its sincerity and legitimacy.

It may seem to us at first legitimate, righteous, and even compassionate. What is more honorable or compassionate, we might think, than his request to see his brothers adequately warned against their terrible danger?

It is actually wicked in its implications. This is so because it implies that the rich man himself had not sufficient warning of the danger of hell to his soul. Further warning than he had received was (he implied) necessary.

The Initial Assertion of This Teaching (Luke 16:29)

In response to the rich man's seemingly legitimate request, Abraham replies that they already have Moses and the prophets to warn them of their danger. Several things about Abraham's response deserve comment.

This response may strike us as harsh, blunt, and unfeeling. We may feel that Abraham's refusal of the rich man's request lacks compassion.

Yet it comes from Abraham—the one who is in heaven—and is really, though indirectly, the teaching of Jesus. Thus, we dare not think that this response is in any way to be faulted.

When Abraham speaks of Moses and the prophets, he uses the common designation of the Old Testament Scriptures—all the Bible completed to that time (Matt. 5:17; 7:12; 11:13; Luke 16:16; John. 1:45; Acts 13:15; 24:14; 28:23; Rom. 3:21; Luke 16:29, 31; 24:27; Acts 26:22).

The clear implication is that the Old Testament is sufficient warning to men even of the unspeakable danger of hell.

If the Old Testament was a sufficient warning to men by itself, then certainly the Old Testament perfected and fulfilled in the New Testament is super-sufficient warning.

The Plain Contradiction of This Teaching (Luke 16:30)

The rich man's response to Abraham is swift, strong, and very negative. The rich man is quite sure that, if his brothers were warned by someone returning to them from the dead, this would be a more sufficient warning. He believes that as a consequence of this better warning they would repent.

Now we see more plainly the rebellion of the rich man. The man in hell contradicts the man in heaven—Abraham, the father of the faithful himself!

We also see more plainly what the rich man wants—one returning from the dead, a miracle of resurrection and the preaching of a resurrected man.

Imagine the impact such a miracle would have. Suppose you could tell your unconverted friend to meet you at the local cemetery late some dark night. Suppose there you could summon one from the dead to assure your skeptical friend that hell was real and that he needed to repent. That would convince him, you might be tempted to think. Yet, Jesus affirms that such a miracle would not convince one who has rejected the light and self-witness of the Scriptures. What an amazing assertion!

The Expanded Declaration of This Teaching (Luke 16:31)
In response to the strong contradiction of the rich man Jesus puts a response in the mouth of Abraham that expands on His previous teaching. Notice four things about it.

Plain Teaching
The evidence or authentication provided by the Scriptures to the divine origin of the their message is not in principle different in its efficacy than the evidence that one would give who came back from the dead. How awesome is the power of Scripture to attest itself to us! What must be the power of the Scriptures to authenticate themselves to us?

Clear Implication
The implication of Jesus' teaching is plain. The depravity by which men reject the Scripture would be sufficient to reject the miraculous light of one returning from the dead. Men need new eyes—not more light! Their problem is the sinful hardness of their hearts to sense and feel the truth.

Underlying Assumption
The message of the Bible authenticates itself in the consciences of all who hear it. It needs no other evidences or added miracles beyond

itself to make men obliged to believe its message. John Calvin in his
Institutes of the Christian Religion makes this point clearly.

> But, with regard to the question, How shall we be persuaded of its
> divine original, unless we have recourse to the decree of the Church?
> This is just as if any one should inquire, How shall we learn to
> distinguish light from darkness, white from black, sweet from bitter?
> For the Scripture exhibits as clear evidence of its truth, as white
> and black things do of their colour, or sweet and bitter things of
> their taste.[1]

Biblical Confirmation

Many other texts in the Bible confirm the teaching of Luke 16:27-31.
The Bible everywhere asserts that the Scriptures are never to be viewed
as a dead letter, but as the living Word of God (Jer. 23:28, 29; John
6:63; Acts 7:38; 1 Peter 1:23-25; and Heb. 4:12, 13). Without closely-
reasoned, lengthy arguments about them or external evidence being
added to them, the Scriptures are sufficient to warrant the infallible
confidence in their truthfulness required for saving faith (Deut. 31:11-
13; John 20:31; Gal. 1:8, 9; Mark 16:15, 16). If one does not assign to
the Scriptures the ability to compel belief in and of themselves, one
raises serious questions about the doctrine of the sufficiency of the
Scriptures (2 Tim. 3:16, 17). If the Scriptures are not sufficient for this
most fundamental of spiritual issues, are they sufficient for anything?

CONCLUSION

Let me allow the great Puritan, John Owen, to put the capstone on
what I have been saying about Luke 16:27-31:

> But is it of this authority and efficacy in itself? See Luke 16:27-31 .
> . . . The question here between Abraham and the rich man in this
> parable,--indeed between the wisdom of God and the superstitious
> contrivances of men,--is about the way and means of bringing those
> who are unbelievers and impenitent unto faith and repentance. He
> who was in hell apprehended that nothing would make them believe
> but a miracle, one rising from the dead and speaking unto them;
> which, or the like marvelous operations, many at this day think
> would have mighty power and influence upon them to settle their
> minds and change their lives. Should they see one "rise from the

dead," and come and converse with them, this would convince them of the immortality of the soul, of future rewards and punishments, as giving them sufficient evidence thereof, so that they would assuredly repent and change their lives; but as things are stated, they have no sufficient evidence of these things, so that they doubt so far about them as that they are not really influenced by them. Give them but one real miracle, and you shall have them forever. This, I say, was the opinion and judgment of him who was represented as in hell, as it is of many who are posting thither apace. He who was in heaven thought otherwise; wherein we have the immediate judgment of Jesus Christ given in this matter, determining this controversy. The question is about sufficient evidence and efficacy to cause us to believe things divine and supernatural; and this he determines to be in the written word, "Moses and the prophets." If he that will not, on the single evidence of the written word, believe [it--SW] to be from God, or a divine revelation of his will, will never believe upon the evidence of miracles nor any other motives, then that written word contains in itself the entire formal reason of faith, or all that evidence of the authority and truth of God in it which faith divine and supernatural rests upon; that is, it is to be believed for its own sake. But saith our Lord Jesus Christ himself, "If men will not hear," that is, believe, "Moses and the prophets, neither will they be persuaded, though one rose from the dead," and come and preach unto them,--a greater miracle than which they could not desire. Now, this could not be spoken if the Scripture did not contain in itself the whole entire formal reason of believing; for if it have not this, something necessary unto believing would be wanting, though that were enjoyed. And this is directly affirmed . . . [2]

PRACTICAL APPLICATIONS

First, in the teaching of Jesus we have an answer to the claims of Roman Catholicism.

Do you know how the Roman Catholic Church claims to show that the Bible is the Word of God? They claim to prove the authority of the Bible from the infallible authority of the Roman Catholic Church vested in the Pope. This is, in fact, one of their great arguments for the authority of the church over the souls of men. They tell Protestants, "Without the church you would not even have your Bible or know that it is God's Word." They ask, "How will you know the divine origin of the Bible, if the church does not tell you?"

What is the answer to this seemingly powerful argument? It is simply that the Word of God needs no one and no church to authorize or authenticate it. It authenticates itself. God speaks in the Word. His message shows itself to be the power and wisdom of God. Remember the words of Calvin quoted before:

> But, with regard to the question, How shall we be persuaded of its divine original, unless we have recourse to the decree of the Church? This is just as if any one should inquire, How shall we learn to distinguish light from darkness, white from black, sweet from bitter? For the Scripture exhibits as clear evidence of its truth, as white and black things do of their colour, or sweet and bitter things of their taste.[3]

Second, in the teaching of Jesus we have an answer to the popularity of the Charismatic movement.

The Continuationist movement is sometimes called the "power-religion" movement. It says that the problem with the church is its lack of powerful miracles. People need to see miracles, signs, and mighty works and then they will believe. Here in our passage we have Jesus' answer to that view. The Word of God is alive, powerful, sufficient, and self-authenticating enough to warn people about the danger of hell and guide them to salvation. No further miracle is needed. Jesus teaches that even miracles that would go way beyond those offered by these movements will not help those who demand a sign. Such demand for a miraculous authentication of the gospel is, in fact, evil. Jesus in another place declares, "But He answered and said to them, 'An evil and adulterous generation craves for a sign; and yet no sign shall be given to it but the sign of Jonah the prophet' " (Matt. 12:39).

Third, in the teaching of Jesus we have an answer to the confusion of evangelicals.

Evangelicals seem to be running to one teaching, program, or theory after another in an attempt to appeal to men. There is no answer in all this. What is needed first and foremost is the preaching and teaching of the powerful Word of God! Evangelicals need to understand and have confidence in the proclamation of the living Word of God and its power to bring men before the judgment seat of God and then to the cross of Christ.

Fourth, in the teaching of Jesus we have an answer to the needs of men.
Moses and the prophets, and Jesus and the apostles—the entire Word of God—proclaim the God of creation, the guilt of men, and the Gospel of God. It is the crucified Christ proclaimed as the wisdom and power of God that is the message which meets the deepest needs of sinful men.

A convincing argument against the continuation of the miraculous gifts need not leave us feeling bereft of power or anxious that the glory has departed. The life, power, glory, and sufficiency for the church in today's world may be found in a renewed confidence in the message of the Christ found in the Scriptures.

1   John Calvin, *The Institutes of the Christian Religion,* trans. John Allen (Phila-
    delphia: Presbyterian Board of Christian Education, n. d.), 1:7:2

2   John Owen, *Works* (London: Banner of Truth Trust, 1968), 4:75-76.

3   Calvin, *Insitutes*, 1:7:2.

SAMUEL E. WALDRON holds a Th.D from Grand Rapids Baptist Seminary and a Ph.D from Southern Seminary in Louisville, Kentucky. He is pastor of Heritage Baptist Church in Owensboro, Kentucky and Professor of Systematic Theology at The Midwest Center for Theological Studies. He and his wife, Charlene, have been married for 30 years and have been blessed with four children.